117

By Katie Swenson

Photography by Harry Connolly

DESIGN WITH LOVE

At Home in America

SCHIFFER PUBLISHING

4880 Lower Valley Road • Atglen, PA 19310

ZIP System

Contents

"Love is space. It is developing our own capacity for spaciousness within ourselves to allow others to be as they are. That is love. And that doesn't mean that we don't have hopes or wishes that things are changed or shifted, but that to come from a place of love is to be in acceptance of what is, even in the face of moving it towards something that is more whole, more just, more spacious for all of us."

—angel Kyodo williams[1]

Foreword

The Enterprise Rose Architectural Fellowship was conceived of in August 1999. It was a time of great optimism. The Soviet Union had fallen, and democracy had taken root in dozens of countries where it had been repressed for decades. The United States had a surplus budget and was paying down debt. The president was talking about infrastructure investments. It was anticipated that the new millennium would bring even more equality, democracy, environmental improvement, and perhaps even peace.

My father, Frederick P. Rose, was one of the optimists. He was born in 1924 to a father who was a small businessperson by trade and an artist by avocation, and a mother who devotedly translated books into braille by hand. From the very beginning, even when they were poor, his family was philanthropic. A sense of the common good was in his DNA. Fred was exceptionally bright and skipped several grades, entering Yale in 1940 at the age of sixteen, the first of his family to go to college. There he encountered both an expanded world—for example, taking a music class with Paul Hindemith—and the contracted world of discrimination against Jews, whose admission was limited by a quota. Eager to serve in the war against fascism, he joined the ROTC, graduated in three years, and enlisted in the navy.

After the war, Fred joined his father and uncle's growing real-estate firm and became a leading New York builder. He loved the design and building process, walking the jobs, speaking to the workers, and frequently visiting his architects' offices, to see not only the progress of his own projects, but what they were designing for his competitors.

As his career and prestige grew, he joined the boards leading New York arts, cultural, and educational institutions, and oversaw the design and construction of their projects, working with architects including Edward Larabee Barns, Kevin Roche, Jim Polsheck, and others. His final project was the American Museum of Natural History's Frederick P. and Sandra P. Rose Center for Earth and Space.

At the end of my father's life, a few weeks before he passed away, he asked me to help him create a fellowship program for young architects. Fred wanted them to be able to get out of the office, and to be liberated from the menial jobs that came with starting in the profession. I wanted them to learn how to be community developers, to work with community development organizations, to learn how to finance and build community solutions, to bring design to places that the design world had forgotten. Out of these two streams, we co-created the vision of what was then called the Frederick P. Rose Architectural Fellowship, to be hosted by Enterprise Community Partners. It was the last of my father's extraordinary philanthropic projects.

Enterprise Community Partners was founded by Jim and Patty Rouse as a national intermediary to grow affordable-housing and community development solutions by partnering with local not-for-profits. Jim Rouse was a hero and occasional mentor of

Opposite: Downtown View, Minneapolis, a project of Abbie Loosen, Rose Fellow 2008–2011. Developer: Project for Pride in Living (PPL) and YouthLink; Architect: UrbanWorks Architecture

YOUTHLINK

mine, and by 1999 I was deeply involved with the organization. At that time, it had a national network of more than 2,000 community development organizations, and a strong technical-assistance group. Today, Enterprise is one of the leading forces of thought leadership, advocacy, and financing in the field of affordable-housing development, bringing more than $6 billion a year to its partners and leading the advancement of community development practice.

Launched in 2000, the Rose Fellowship was initially a three-year partnership, and now a two-year one, among Enterprise, the fellow, and the host organization. Enterprise helps recruit hosts and candidates and provides the curriculum, support, and funding for the program. Community partners apply to host a fellow, detailing their aspirations for organizational ambitions and a work plan.

Enterprise also understood the need for emerging architects to use the time in the fellowship toward their licensure, and designed a program with appropriate mentorship to help achieve that. In the early days, the fellows were all architects. But in recent years, the program has expanded to include landscape architects and artists who have a passion for community development and who proposed meaningful work projects in conjunction with local community development organizations. The first group of fellows' work ranged from an award-winning Native American community in New Mexico to a rural housing-project model in Hale County, Alabama, one of the poorest in America. It quickly became the premier social-action design fellowship in the field.

The results of the optimism of 1999 have been mixed. While globally there has been an extraordinary reduction in poverty and increase in wealth, the distribution of that wealth has been more and more unequal. Civilization is increasingly urbanizing, and staggering into climate volatility, drunk on fossil fuels. Natural disasters, human oppression, violence, and corruption have escalated migrations, which have given rise to nativism as a counterreaction. In the United States, as in many other countries, the tensions between those who seek transformation toward an imagined better world versus those who seek regression to an imagined previous world have frozen governments, which are unable to address the existential issues they are facing.

However, the communities in which the Enterprise Rose Fellows work are eager for action, committed to democratically founded positive change, and brimming with creativity. Working in the forgotten rural and urban neighborhoods of America, the Rose Fellows are creating models of a better world. They were among the first to design deeply green affordable housing, ranging from straw-bale homes on Indian reservations to inner-city multifamily projects. They led the imagining of transit-oriented development and transit corridors. They figured out how to bring social, health, and educational services to the communities in which they worked. They helped revitalize retail corridors. They built housing for low-income seniors, people with disabilities, and much more. And every project soared on the wings of beauty.

Some Enterprise Rose Fellows have remained in the communities to which their fellowships brought them. Others have gone on to be significant leaders in the field elsewhere. And so, the fellowship provides multiple benefits, creating tangible projects, empowering and enriching communities, and growing extraordinary leaders.

The works that the fellows, their community development hosts, and their communities' residents have created are models of emergent solutions to the issues of social justice, income inequality, and environmental destruction. These are particularly powerful forces in lower-income communities. To overcome them requires the equally powerful force of collective vision, manifested through design, finance, development, and construction skills. But, as so beautifully written about by Katie Swenson and photographed by Harry Connolly in this book, it also requires deep listening, collaboration, and love.

Martin Luther King Jr. said, "Power without love is reckless and abusive, and love without power is sentimental and anemic. Power at its best is love implementing the demands of justice, and justice at its best is power correcting everything that stands against love."

Love is most powerful in its collective form. The solutions to the issues of our age lie in cultures of pervasive altruism.

Katie Swenson embodies the power of love, expressed through design. She was one of the program's earliest fellows, building affordable housing and engaging in community development work in Charlottesville, Virginia. When she became the fellowship program's executive director, the fellowship was at an inflection point. Enterprise had to commit to the value of the program and ensuring its continuation. With her own firsthand experience in Charlottesville, and an understanding of the impact the program was making in her fellows' communities, Katie endeavored to demonstrate the value of the program, raising both the awareness and the funds to allow it to flourish to this day. Building on the lessons of the Rose Fellows, she expanded the scope of Enterprise's design work to include the Affordable Housing Design Leadership Institute and the Cultural and Climate Resilience Program, all the while advocating tirelessly for the incorporation of design excellence and the power of creativity into all of Enterprise's work.

Throughout her term of leadership, Katie traveled the country, mentoring fellows and their community development partners; bringing tools, resources, and appreciation for their efforts; and learning from them how to be an effective advocate for better affordable housing and community design. The beauty of this book flows from the intimacy of her relationship with the people and work that it describes.

May the work of the Enterprise Rose Fellows continue to grow the seed of beloved communities, and from them, might the common good flourish.

—Jonathan F. P. Rose

Introduction

In my final year of architecture school, I heard the term "community architect" for the first time. I had never heard those two words together, but something in me immediately lit up: whatever a community architect was, *that's* what I wanted to be.

The source of those words was Enterprise Community Partners, which was issuing a call for its first offering of what was then known as the Frederick P. Rose Architectural Fellowship. Named for Frederick P. Rose, a developer and philanthropist who believed in the value of good design and the spirit of public service, the Enterprise Rose Fellowship provides grants for local housing organizations to host an emerging designer for three years to help underresourced communities reach ambitious development goals.

In addition to financial resources, Rose Fellows are given access to Enterprise's national support network and the time to become immersed in a community. The goal is to give the fellows a chance to get to know the people and understand their unique circumstances and needs. After learning from the local community and developing trusting relationships, these fellows contribute their design skills to help create sustainable, equitable, connected communities for people of all income levels.

In short, the fellowship is a platform for social-justice designers to learn how to become community architects. And this sounded exactly like what I wanted to do. Throughout my teens and twenties I had volunteered with housing and homeless organizations, where I witnessed the slippery slope of housing insecurity and its devastating effects on individuals and families. I went to architecture school because I loved design, and I had a vague notion of wanting to be involved in the creation of beautiful and stable, affordable housing. Shortly after graduating from the University of Virginia School of Architecture, I applied to be a Rose Fellow with the Piedmont Housing Alliance (Piedmont Housing) in Charlottesville, Virginia, and was accepted into the class of 2001–2004. I knew little about the world of community development, and less about exactly what I was signing up for. I had two toddlers at home: my daughters Sophie and Olivia were four and one, respectively, and their sister, Bliss, would be born while I was in the third year of the fellowship.

It was a challenging time, to say the least. Navigating the demands of family with the challenges and aspirations of the fellowship was energizing, at times overwhelming, and often humbling. Ultimately, it was life changing.

As with all Rose Fellows, I stepped into a community development initiative that was already underway. My primary project was the 10th and Page Street Neighborhood Revitalization Initiative.[1] My role was to participate in the project management and funding

Opposite: Tsigo Bugeh Village, Ohkay Owingeh, New Mexico, a project of Jamie Blosser, Rose Fellow 2000–2003. Developer: Ohkay Owingeh Housing Authority; Architects: Van Amburgh+Parés+Co. Architects and Ned Cherry

Katie Swenson, Rose Fellow, 2001–2004, photo from 2005

while designing and overseeing the rehabilitation or new construction of thirty-one homes—about 10 percent of the neighborhood—for mixed-income homeownership.

The 10th and Page Street neighborhood is in the center of Charlottesville, halfway between the Downtown Mall and the University of Virginia. It is near Vinegar Hill, which had been a thriving African American, mixed-use neighborhood until the 1960s, when the Charlottesville Redevelopment and Housing Authority (CHRA) demolished it as part of an urban renewal program. Many Vinegar Hill residents were offered relocation in West Haven, CHRA's new, 126-unit rental development adjacent to 10th and Page.

The roots of its problems run deep. Charlottesville was too small to have been one of more than 239 US cities that had a Home Owners' Loan Corporation residential security map—now known as redlining maps. Nonetheless, the racialized real-estate practices of the time, coupled with federally mandated underwriting requirements that promoted segregated housing, restricted access to people of color. Tenth and Page was one of a few areas where the black and brown community could live. However, it eventually suffered from the same type of disinvestment and displacement seen in other redlined areas, particularly as subsequent urban renewal programs disrupted the socio-spatial fabric. According to Mapping Inequality, "As homeownership was arguably the most significant means of intergenerational wealth building in the United States in the twentieth century, these redlining practices from eight decades ago had long-term effects in creating wealth inequalities that we still see today."[2]

By 2000, decades of disinvestment had left the area with a series of challenges. Piedmont Housing, the City of Charlottesville, and a local advisory group prepared to respond to goals stated by residents in the Neighborhood Comprehensive Plan. The top four priorities were to preserve neighborhood stability by improving housing conditions and striking a balance between renters and homeowners; improve deteriorating housing conditions and address consequent crime that undermines quality of life and morale; acknowledge that some residents no longer feel safe in the neighborhood, especially at night; and embrace community involvement and empowerment as critical to improving the neighborhood.

When I started my fellowship, there were a few houses still standing on the corner of 10th and Page. They were slated for demolition, but it was taking some time. I heard there had been a double homicide in a dilapidated house on the northwest corner of the intersection, and the police chief and many residents (as I understood) wanted it torn down. Also slated for demolition was the house on the southwest corner, which was empty but had recently been occupied by a family with five children. The house reeked of mold and there was no railing on the stairs.

I had the idea that I would open a "design center" in the house on the southwest corner, since my vision of being a Rose Fellow meant spending as much time in the neighborhood as possible. I cannot remember anyone protesting. I hung sheets of Homasote wall board in what used to be the living room, and painted the first floor white. Despite my temporary renovation efforts—and even after I closed off the kitchen and bathroom—I could not get rid of the mold smell. I moved a desk and computer in and started hanging maps, drawings, and neighborhood research on the walls.

Within two weeks, I got a call informing me that someone had broken into the house. It was about 4 p.m., which was when I had to pick up my daughter Sophie at daycare. With her in a car seat in the back, I drove over to the house. I kept a drill and basic tools in the trunk of my car, and I knew there were a few sheets of plywood around the corner. A neighbor helped me screw the plywood over the door and broken windows.

That night, after I put Sophie and her baby sister Liv to bed, I was struck by the events of the day. We lived only 2 miles away, but my street was safe. I was in my newly renovated 1925 farmhouse, and my babies were asleep in their beds. I thought about the mother of five who had recently moved, and wondered where she and her children had gone.

While I knew less than I know now about racial inequity, it was no mystery that we owed our safety and well-being, in part, to being white. I thought I could do something to make things better and naively thought that design could be the answer.

Realizing that the design center was not a good idea, I moved my office into a local architecture firm. But I showed up in the neighborhood every day to work on behalf of the project's steering group. Over time, as I began to form relationships with the residents, I realized that this job didn't require me to be an expert; it required me to be humble and a facilitator.

It was a mistake to think that design by itself could solve a problem, without recognizing that it takes people, joining together and using many tools, including design, to support their community. I learned what it meant to be an outsider in a community, even one so close to home, and how persistent race and class divisions can define a city.

This experience, however, also committed me more fundamentally to strive for the core values I hold today: that everyone, no matter their race or the neighborhood they live in, deserves a well-designed, affordable home in a safe community. My experience as a Rose Fellow strengthened my commitment to making that aspiration a reality. It also raised an essential question: Could effective community design help overcome the trauma born from years of racism, disinvestment, and neglect? On an individual level, could I learn to recognize the power dynamic of my personal privilege in a way that allowed me to contribute to the dismantling of systemic injustice, rather than contributing to its perpetuation?

The other eight Rose Fellows from the first two classes were on their own fellowship journey, and we provided a support network to each other through this transformative time. We organized monthly check-in calls and shared our project work plans. We were the only designers in our host organizations and were trying to figure out how to be most effective in our unconventional roles.

One of my Rose Fellow colleagues, Jamie Blosser, was working with Ohkay Owingeh Housing Authority in Ohkay Owingeh, New Mexico. In 2001, she planned the first all-fellows retreat at her site. As soon as I got to Ohkay Owingeh Pueblo, the vast open spaces and the terra-cotta landscape, so different from the East Coast, where I'd spent most of my life, made me feel relaxed and expansive. During the weeklong retreat, the nine of us had ample time to trade stories of successes and setbacks. Everyone was confronting complex environments, and I realized I was not alone in feeling overwhelmed. Over the course of that week, we dug into our projects and

Diane and Louis Baskfield, homeowners on Anderson Street, 10th and Page Street neighborhood, Charlottesville, VA, photo from 2005

problem-solved together. The "fellowship of the fellowship," as we called it, gave us a way to learn from and support each other. By the time I left New Mexico, I felt fortified to get back to work.

When my fellowship concluded, I had become substantially more experienced and aware and chose to remain in the community I'd grown to love. With a team of collaborators, I opened the Charlottesville Community Design Center, where we endeavored to apply the community-led approach to neighborhoods across the city.

Two years later, Enterprise Community Partners hired me as director of the Rose Fellowship program. Here was the opportunity to continue working at the intersection of architecture and affordable housing. I was now in a position to give back to the program that had set me on this path, to mentor—and learn from—the next generation of emerging designers and architects.

Over the next twelve years, I would travel the country to recruit and support communities and fellows. I have visited with Rose Fellows at every stage of their tenure, from the early, optimistic days, to the days when the work seemed insurmountable, to the moments of celebration as their team broke ground on a new affordable-housing development, to the long-anticipated day the first residents moved in. Perhaps more important, I got to know the people who form the backbone of the community development field, many of whom have dedicated their lives to the locations they serve.

This work with the Rose Fellows and Enterprise Community Partners has been an incredible privilege. I could never have predicted how completely it would change my life, both personally and professionally. The Rose Fellowship provided the initial platform that enabled me to test out and refine the inchoate notions I had about what it means to be a community architect.

It taught me how to approach design first from a place of listening. It sparked a revolution in my thinking about how designers and community developers can work collaboratively to address the deeper issues preventing communities from enjoying equal access to every kind of opportunity—issues as seemingly intractable as systemic poverty, institutionalized racism, crime, neglect, and abandonment.

As the fellowship begins its third decade, eighty-six Rose Fellows have designed and developed nearly 40,000 homes in partnership with local groups in forty states in the US and Puerto Rico. In border towns, inner-city streets, rural communities, Rust Belt cities, remote tribal reservations, and neighborhoods starved for resources, the fellows have learned how to navigate the complex and sensitive process of entering a community as an outsider and finding the best ways to be helpful.

Across the nation, 19 million families—about one in six US families—face housing insecurity. Most of the communities in which the fellows have worked have been communities of color. According to 2018 US census data, the highest poverty rate by race is found among Native Americans (25.4%). Blacks (20.8%) have the second-highest poverty rate, and Hispanics (of any race) have the third-highest poverty rate (17.6%). Both whites and Asians have a poverty rate of 10.1%.[3]

The architecture profession, however, is about 80 percent male and 80 percent white. In the first two classes, we were eight white and one Mexican-born American, and we were six men and three women. Today, fellowship cohorts are more representative of the general population, with an even number of men and women, and at least half are people of color, Diversity in the program disrupts a view of architecture predicated on the idea of white professionals working with primarily white corporate and institutional clients. The increasing diversity of the fellow cohort means that everyone learns from an ever-broadening spectrum of experiences and perspectives.

In anticipation of the Rose Fellowship's twentieth anniversary, photographer Harry Connolly and I embarked on a two-year journey to visit Rose Fellows all over America. The result is this book, which shares the stories of ten diverse fellowship locations, capturing best practices and hard won wisdom. I first met Harry in 2005 when he came to photograph our work in Charlottesville. He has now met and photographed every fellow in the program, along with hundreds of community members.

Harry is as much a storyteller as a visual artist, and the subjects of his photos are often people whose stories usually remain untold. The writing reflects my personal perspective, and I have tried to represent each person's experiences and aspirations authentically. In doing so, I have become increasingly aware of the problematic nature of telling other people's stories through my lens as a white person who has never known discrimination, housing insecurity, or economic hardship. I could not have done so without their generous cooperation and support. Each person featured in *Design with Love* welcomed us into their communities and spent many hours with us, and each has participated in the telling and editing of their stories.

As our travels wrapped up and Harry and I began poring over transcripts and notes, we noticed that people described their work in remarkably similar ways. It became clear that the most-successful communities—and fellows—were those that share the same core elements: a clear commitment to their mission, a common understanding of the philosophical and spiritual underpinnings of their work, and the tenacity to meet their community's goals.

Chief among these core values was love. That's right, love. Love is not a word often used in architecture circles, yet it has enormous implications for the work of architects and designers. The Greeks spoke of eight types of love: *eros*, erotic love; *philia*, affectionate love; *storge*, familiar love; *ludus*, playful love; *mania*, obsessive love; *pragm*, enduring love; *philautia*, self-love; and, most important for us, *agape*—unconditional, selfless love, the highest and most radical type.

This is the love that Dr. Martin Luther King Jr. used as a tool of urban design for what he called the Beloved Community. "In the Beloved Community," he said, "poverty, hunger and homelessness will not be tolerated because international standards of human decency will not allow it. Racism and all forms of discrimination, bigotry, and prejudice will be replaced by an all-inclusive spirit of sisterhood and brotherhood."[4]

I have come to believe that love is as crucial a tool for design as solving spatial problems, meeting a pro forma, or getting a building permit. The social critic Dr. Cornel West reminds us, however, that love without justice is sentimentality. "Never forget that justice is what love looks like in public," says West.[5]

The love expressed through direct service is a first step. This means the work of design but also the work of listening, valuing a variety of perspectives, and building trusting relationships. It recognizes that residents themselves are the experts in

Katie Swenson (front row, fourth from left), with Rose Fellows and advisors at the Institute for Contemporary Art, Boston

understanding their own needs, aspirations, and solutions. Too often, architects enter a community with the attitude that as the professional, they know best what that community needs. The foundation for collaborative design is based on two-way, long-term community relationships, increasing exponentially both the number of problems that can be solved and the number of people who can benefit.

In the most-successful partnerships, the Rose Fellows bring their whole selves to their placements. This, too, is an act of love. They work to recognize the power dynamics of their position and learn about the history and structural forces that have contributed to a community's current experience. They bring professional skills and knowledge, but they do so with a level of empathy and self-reflection that acknowledges their positions as actors, active participants, and collaborators. They learn from their communities in equal measure, and usually more.

Love, too, may be the only force powerful enough to undermine and delegitimize the wide-scale systemic forces that make community development necessary in the first place. We know that without a stable home, everything else falls apart. What will it take for us to create a national housing policy that commits to the fundamental right for every person to have a good-quality home?

As I reflected on twenty years of working in community development, about why things are the way they are and what we can do, it occurred to me that maybe we simply don't love enough. We care for the people we know, but we neglect to recognize the essential humanity of people who are different from us or those we may never meet. We neglect to understand that their essential humanity is just as worthy as ours. And it is connected to ours.

This is why love matters—in policy, architecture, community development, and our everyday lives. None of this work can be accomplished unless we consider each member of the greater community a member of our own community.

The work of the Rose Fellows and their local partners represents the myriad ways that people are bringing about Dr. King's Beloved Community. During this journey, I heard the quote, "Love is advocating relentlessly on behalf of your community." While you will meet many of the Rose Fellows here, their host community members are relentlessly, over decades, making the seemingly impossible things possible. They are the people who get insurmountable things done. Person by person, home by home, neighborhood by neighborhood, together they are doing the hard, messy work of moving the housing industry forward.

I hope this book will give you an appreciation for the results the Rose Fellows have achieved, and for the diversity and beauty of the communities that have welcomed them.

And, I hope it will inspire you to get to work wherever you are, to join the legions of committed designers, developers, community organizers, and neighbors fighting to bring justice home.

San Ysidro, California

"Families are not governed by borders," says Rose Fellow David Flores, "they are governed by love. Familial ties that have lived across the border go back four or five generations now. We like to say that the border is really the best of both."

South of downtown San Diego and north of Tijuana lies the small border town of San Ysidro. Long home to working-class people focused on advancing civil rights and improving education and economic stability, this is the place where influential advocates such as Cesar Chavez, Juanita Ruiz, Carlos Perez, and Herman Baca came to organize.

San Ysidro is home to about 30,000 permanent residents and looks and behaves like any small town. One can walk the span of the historic district in fifteen minutes, passing parks, the public library, restaurants, churches, and a lively downtown commercial district.

But it is also home to one of the busiest land-border crossings in the world. Each day, tens of thousands of people flow between the United States and Mexico through the San Ysidro Land Port of Entry, which facilitates the passage of forty-seven million people a year.

Less than 5 miles apart, San Ysidro and Tijuana are intricately connected. While the street signs in San Ysidro are in English, Spanish is spoken on every corner, and for decades people have traveled back and forth between the two towns to shop, visit family, attend school, receive medical care, and work. Many people at the border consider themselves binational citizens. Families go back four or five generations, often including both Mexican and American citizens and siblings with different citizenship statuses.

David was in the second-year Rose Fellowship class, moving to San Ysidro nearly twenty years ago to begin his fellowship at Casa Familiar (Casa), a social service organization that provides more than forty bilingual programs and services at six sites. He never left.

David became Casa's community development director following his fellowship and focuses on addressing the holistic needs of border community members—the design and construction of affordable housing, local parks, arts and community centers, and creating spaces for legal counseling on immigration issues.

Opposite: Sculpture: *Of a Leaf or a Feather*; Artist: Norie Sato, covering a section of the south-bound pedestrian walkway to Mexico on the east side of the San Ysidro Land Port of Entry

The border between the US and Mexico was first drawn after the Mexican-American War ended in 1848. While there has always been a barbed wire marking the boundary, for the first hundred years the border remained porous. People traveled back and forth with relative ease, with families meeting on either side to spend time with one another. Jorge Cordova, a long-time San Ysidro resident now in his sixties, recounts that in

MEXICO

Katie Swenson and David Flores, Border Field State Park, the space between the existing border fence and new "wall," only accessible by DHS and Border Patrol, San Diego

Southbound Pedestrian Walkway at PedEast, San Ysidro Port of Entry, opened 2018

his teenage years, people would routinely walk across, no identification required, no hassles or wait time.

"If we felt like having some tacos, we'd pitch in for money and somebody would take off, and he'd be back in fifteen, twenty minutes at the most," he says. "The tacos would still be warm."

That scenario is almost impossible to imagine now. By the 1990s, the Clinton administration intensified national focus on illegal immigration, and a new 14-mile fence along the US-Mexico border near San Ysidro was built as part of Operation Gatekeeper. After 9/11, tightening border security at all US ports of entry was top priority, with every border crossing becoming increasingly militarized.

Congress passed the REAL ID Act in 2005, stipulating a double fence along the entire US-Mexico boundary, equipped with barbed wire, sensors, and surveillance cameras and stretching all the way into the Pacific Ocean. In 2009, the Department of Homeland Security closed down Friendship Park in San Diego, which Pat Nixon had inaugurated in the 1970s as a symbol of US-Mexican binational friendship, and a short time later, a third 20-foot wall of steel bars was installed along the border. By early 2012, the border fence was extended an additional 300 feet into the ocean, resulting in its westernmost expansion.

Like many communities, San Ysidro needs better schools, improved infrastructure, more public transit, affordable housing, and street lighting for security. But the massive flow of people through the town each day affects everything from the economy to city planning. Most of San Ysidro's federal resources are siphoned away from the local community, directed instead toward improving highways and security, especially at the port of entry.

Casa Familiar tries to bridge this gap by providing supportive services to border residents. And David Flores is uniquely suited to contribute. He has lived his entire life at the border, navigating life on both sides and helping others do the same.

David was born in Juarez, Mexico, and immigrated to Texas at age nine, when his father and aunt successfully petitioned their entry in 1980. However, when David was nineteen, his father was deported following an arrest. His father served time in an American prison, and upon his release, he was forced to go back to Mexico. His father's deportation, David says, permanently altered the fabric of his family.

"I couldn't believe it," he says. "To find yourself in a place where the whole source of income for your family and stability is removed from one day to the next was daunting. It completely changed my perspective about my future because I knew from that moment on that there's nobody else I could count on. My brother, my sister, and I automatically knew we needed to be independent and figure things out."

David and his siblings did figure things out, but his mother's dreams of home and family shattered. "From that moment on, she's always felt like a wanderer, not really belonging anywhere," says David. His parents, still married, live on different sides of the border.

During this tumultuous time, David put himself through architecture school. In high school he had learned to draft and fell in love with the challenge of putting pencil to paper to produce precise drawings. "It was hard for me to go through [architecture

David Flores, Rose Fellow,
2001–2004

rge Cordova, resident,
n Ysidro

school] and push myself to design—to let loose, to wander and dream of molding space and place—and not think of how to be practical because of the harsh realities of life," David says.

That is, until his capstone project. "By then," he says, "I recognized the border as the place that I should engage with all of my experience and life being split between the US and Mexico. Architecture became for me a mission. To help change the experience of the border, of a border community that should highlight the best of what it means to be a binational citizen."

David's vision for the border is that it should be a welcoming place that meets the demands of national security while recognizing that people are conducting everyday life—walking to school, driving to work, going shopping—on both sides, sometimes at great personal cost.

Though the national conversation focuses on illegal border crossings and justifying the need for increasingly militarized security measures, the vast majority of people who travel back and forth across the border do so legally. In David's view, the border should be "only a pause" for them, and his vision is that the architecture at the San Ysidro Port of Entry can make the experience of crossing the border humane and respectful, even pleasant.

This is a bold and ambitious position, given the current stressful—even traumatic—border-crossing experience. The Department of Homeland Security has created a stratified system of access depending on citizenship and residency or visa status. Wait times to cross can climb to five hours or more, resulting in lost sleep, work, study, and time with loved ones—not to mention hours of exposure to the exhaust fumes of thousands of idling vehicles. David believes it doesn't have to be this way, and his work reflects this.

"Architecture became for me a mission. To help change the experience of the border, of a border community that should highlight the best of what it means to be a binational citizen." —David Flores

The $741 million, LEED-certified San Ysidro Port of Entry expansion, completed in December 2019, was one of the largest infrastructure projects in the United States. The port processes 90,000 daily commuters through San Ysidro, one-third of whom cross on foot and two-thirds in vehicles. David's involvement in this construction project is truly inestimable. He advocated changes to the plan of the new facility that would prioritize the experience of the 30,000 pedestrians moving daily through the site's 10-plus acres. He and the Casa Familiar team successfully advocated for the creation of a second pedestrian port of entry, called PedWest, which more than doubles the pedestrian-processing capacity. They also successfully integrated a pedestrian bridge overpass over Interstate 5 to help people get safely from one end of the border station to the other.

Through the US General Service Administration's Art in Architecture Program, David had a hand in selecting artwork that expresses what it means to cross this particular border. He also advocated for a new pedestrian plaza, completed in September 2019, that offers a friendlier welcome to people crossing on foot from Mexico to the US.

A more insidious menace threatens the residents of San Ysidro and Tijuana: air quality from idling vehicles at the border. Casa has installed a dozen air-quality

ulpture: *About Time*; Artist:
arcos Ramirez, known as
RRE; commissioned by
e U.S. General Services
dministration (GSA), San
idro Land Port of Entry

Right and opposite: The United States border crossing, Tijuana, Mexico

UNITED STATES

UNITED STATES

adidas
NISSAN
FRONTIER
WASHINGTON
C85949F
EVERGREEN STATE

SAN YSIDRO PORT OF ENTRY
SAN YSIDRO PORT

sensors that transmit information to San Diego State University and the University of Washington. While this evidence-based collection is happening, an art project interprets the danger in a more visceral way. *Pollution Painting*, displayed on the roof of Casa Familiar's art and design center, The FRONT, is an ongoing project by artist Andy Sturm, created with youth at Casa Familiar's Art Docent program. Using soot that collects on the rinds of a resident's citrus trees over a single day, Sturm draws the word *respirar*—breathe—on canvas, making the amount of soot in the air not just visible but provocative.

These initiatives are essential because a port of entry's primary job is seen as border security, without regard for thoughtful design that would create a positive user experience or urban identity. What's worse, as a federal project, the port is not required to have a Community Benefits Agreement (CBA), which would require the developer to provide specific amenities to the local community in exchange for the opportunity to build.

For example, communities with a CBA in place can require that projects benefit the community by hiring a percentage of local workers, pay a living wage, or contribute to an affordable-housing fund. The unemployment rate in San Ysidro is 16.3 percent, much higher than the national average, but the General Service Administration (GSA) has no legal responsibility to give back to the local economy or to residents—even though this is the largest investment the community will see. At a political level, the amount of money the US government spends on border regulation, while neglecting the needs of the local people, represents a crime of neglect.

Indeed, in recent years the national border conversation has focused on the hideous practice of separating children from their parents. While this extreme injustice represents the utmost cruelty, David and Casa Familiar have another word for what has been happening at the border over the course of many administrations: *community abandonment*. This is the crisis Casa Familiar aims to address.

Under the leadership of CEO Lisa Cuestas, Casa Familiar is changing its vision statement to *Casa Familiar será el líder en la lucha contra el abandono comunitario*: Casa Familiar will lead the fight against community abandonment. "For Casa Familiar, the issue is, How do we continue to provide the most stable environment for families and help them figure out those difficult transitions in order to keep them as healthy as possible? Whether it's health or whether it's immigration processing, whether it's housing assistance or social interaction, then we need to continue to do that."

One of the city's biggest challenges is high-quality, affordable housing. For decades, David has been working on creating homes and neighborhoods that provide stability and safety. His first project as a Rose Fellow was Casitas de la Florecitas, eight affordable single-family homes for first-time homeowners.

These small homes are meticulously maintained, the warmth of their colorful stucco exterior radiating energy. The color scheme—vibrant pinks, greens, blues, and yellows—is not accidental, nor is it purely aesthetic. "There is a beautiful freedom in how color connects you to the places you are from," David says. "When you stand next to a vibrant wall, you feel the color. It's great to have that freedom. Color is life; it changes your perspective."

Casitas de la Florecitas, San Ysidro, CA. Developer: Casa Familiar; Architect: Poster Mirto McDonald Architects and NTD Architects

sa Cuestas, Chief Executive
fficer, Casa Familiar

The use of color in Mexico is a point of pride, and here in San Ysidro it's also a community-organizing tool. David worked to get paint donations and then organized neighbors to help paint other houses on the block. The alley on which the Casitas are located is now clean and safe, with murals—some art, some announcements—that energize and unite the community.

Since this first project, David has directed the design and development of hundreds of homes. The core principles he learned at Casitas remain. The first is that the architecture's cultural expression matters, whether through color and materials or the design of outdoor plazas and landscapes. The second is that engaging residents in the design of places leads to their pride of ownership and the properties' ongoing maintenance—and this can extend to the larger community.

Casa's latest project is an ambitious, mixed-used development nearly twenty years in the making. Located less than a mile from the US-Mexico border, Living Rooms at the Border is a 13,469-square-foot project in the heart of San Ysidro. First conceived in 2001 by the longtime former CEO of Casa, Andrea Skorepa, and designed by architect Teddy Cruz (Estudio Teddy Cruz + Fonna Forman), Living Rooms at the Border contains ten units of affordable housing, office space for Casa Familiar's immigration services, the El K-Fe Barista Youth Training Program, studio space for artists, and a 1,100-square-foot pavilion that the University of California at San Diego will use for a variety of programs. The nearly $10 million project also included the restoration of Our Lady of Mount Carmel Church, built in 1927, and its transformation into El Salon, a multimedia performance space used by theatrical group in residence Teatro Máscara Mágica.

In 2010, Living Rooms at the Border was included in an exhibition at New York's Museum of Modern Art called *Small Scale, Big Change: New Architectures of Social Engagement*. The exhibit featured eleven projects from around the world that brought architecturally compelling and socially valuable developments to underserved communities. It was thrilling to have a model of this innovative project included in the exhibition, but it would be years before the plans became reality.

The long timetable to completion—Living Rooms finally broke ground in December 2018 and was completed in January 2020—reflects the complicated nature of designing, building, and funding an unconventional space—one that doesn't conform to zoning and is built on a small parcel of land. Unit affordability, always a difficult pro forma puzzle, proved to be another major challenge. "Some of the hardest realities were that even though we set a range of affordability for those units, from 40 percent Area Median Income (AMI)[1] to 70 percent AMI, we just kept hearing over and over that they weren't affordable," Lisa says.

The problem was that San Ysidro is included in the city of San Diego's average-median-income calculations. "So the average median income for a family of four is $80,000," Lisa explains, "when really, for some families in San Ysidro, it's more like $30,000." Casa worked with a variety of funding methods and sources to complete the Living Rooms project and to help make the units affordable for San Ysidro residents, including New Markets Tax Credits allocated by Civic San Diego, grants from the PARC Foundation and ARTPLACE America, and the County of San Diego. Financing partners included Capital Impact Partner and Citi Community Capital. Living Rooms

ght and following spread:
ving Rooms at the Border,
n Ysidro, CA. Developer: Casa
miliar; Architect: Estudio
eddy Cruz + Fonna Forman

Arturo and Bertha Ruiz, residents, Casitas de la Florecitas

at the Borders was completed at the end of 2019, and families began moving into their new homes in January 2020.

A few blocks away is Paseo la Paz, a 139-unit building that Casa Familiar helped develop near a new transit stop. This project also faced high affordability hurdles. "When we had community sessions to explain the application process for the 139 units, 700 people showed up over two different sessions—700 people for 139 units," Lisa says. "And then a hundred or maybe 150 of them just walked out when they saw the rents. It was so frustrating. What are we doing, I thought, building housing that people can't afford, and it's called affordable housing?" Casa also spearheaded the design of a pedestrian corridor linking the units to the transit stop. "There's so much that's happening in a very small footprint, and we couldn't think of the project as this thing that has a property line," Lisa says. "It had to be about immediately thinking of how we were going to connect with the surrounding neighborhood."

Caught up in national forces affecting border crossing and immigration policy, and home to generations of binational families that need to live close to the border, San Ysidro faces formidable challenges. But David, now a long-term resident, remains optimistic.

"I like that I can use all the skills that I've obtained up to this point to be able to help people not feel abandoned, people not feel like this is not their home," he says. "I always try to reflect on the fact that the lady doing fitness Zumba classes at Casa Familiar could be my mom. That the senior in the knitting class could be my grandmother, because that's the community I grew up in. Whatever I can do to understand our systems or policy, the way that things happen for a community like San Ysidro, then I'll do whatever I need to do to make sure that this community's voice participates and is heard."

Over the past nearly twenty years, David has translated his own experience of being a transnational, binational citizen into sustained action on behalf of his Beloved Community. He has effectively turned his deep love for his own family, as well as the personal understanding of the effects of family separation, into a life's work of caring for his community.

"Every day that I wake up," David says, "I'll work to stabilize myself, my family unit, my community." His commitment is the very opposite of abandonment. It is an ongoing act of love.

Atlanta, Georgia

"Looking back over my life, I just wasn't really comfortable with what I saw, particularly communities nestled behind downtowns where a lot of resources were on the proverbial wrong side of the railroad tracks," says Leonard Adams, founder of Quest Communities. "Where communities of color didn't have the resources, were underserved and impoverished, with low education, a lack of healthy food, and experiencing a crisis of affordable housing. I always wondered, why? Why is that?"

Design may be the primary tool of community architects, and housing is often their focus. But the ultimate goal is whole-scale justice, and every social need can and should be addressed through design—affordable housing, economic opportunity, access to healthcare and education, and environmental health—to ensure long-term success.

Seen through this lens, community designers are working to bring about Dr. King's "Beloved Community"—a phrase that resounds in Atlanta. Known throughout the world as the birthplace of the civil rights movement, Atlanta was the home of activists who took a bold stand against entrenched forces of systemic racism. Legends such as Dr. Martin Luther King Jr., Coretta Scott King, Andrew Jackson Young Jr., Jesse Hill Jr., and Representative John Lewis made their home here. Their work changed the course of American history.

Thanks to their legacy and the efforts of countless others, Atlanta came to be known as the Black Mecca of the South,[1] the home of some of the nation's most successful black entrepreneurs, entertainers, politicians, investors, and developers. Yet, as is the case throughout America, Atlanta's black and minority communities still suffer greater social inequities than their white neighbors. There is much to be done.

According to a recent study from the Annie E. Casey Foundation, the median household income of Atlanta's African American community is $26,605, while their white counterparts' is more than three times that at $84,944. Meanwhile, 88 percent of white students exceeded Georgia reading standards, while only 24 percent of black students did.[2] Health injustices, which Dr. Martin Luther King Jr. called "the most shocking and inhuman" form of inequality,[3] are no less urgent: African Americans in Atlanta have higher mortality rates than their white neighbors when it comes to illnesses such as HIV/AIDS, stroke, diabetes, prostate cancer, and breast cancer.[4]

Rose Fellow Nick Forest and Quest Community Development Organization are working to improve these conditions. Nick's family hails from the South, and he was already

Nicholas Forest (right), Rose Fellow 2018–2020, with Leonard Adams,
Quest Community Development Organization

doing community-based work in Atlanta when colleagues at the National Organization of Minority Architects (NOMA) encouraged him to apply for a Rose Fellowship.

Nick was a natural fit. "I was too invested in this city and its communities to leave," he says. "One of the things I often thought about when I was working for an architecture firm is that I was designing buildings and structures in other cities, when there were issues in my own backyard that I could be using my skill set to help resolve."

Led by founder, president, and CEO Leonard Adams, Quest's main office is in Westside, about 3 miles from where Dr. King grew up and served as co-pastor at Ebenezer Baptist Church. His legacy remains a potent presence. But it's also still experiencing some of the gravest effects of redlining, a discriminatory practice by which a financial institution—often with federal backing—refused to offer loans, mortgages, credit, insurance, or other financial services to people in low-income communities.

Maps made in 1938 by the Home Owners' Loan Corporation (HOLC) of Atlanta, as well as 238 other US cities, determined the "mortgage security" of neighborhoods, primarily on the basis of the color of its inhabitants. Black and other minority communities typically received D ratings; considered as "hazardous" because of decades of disinvestment, the areas where Quest focuses its efforts are now ripe for gentrification.[5]

"According to recent research, Atlanta's Westside neighborhoods are among the most challenging in the US for achieving upward economic mobility," says Jaren Abedania, vice president of real estate at the Westside Future Fund (WFF). "Presently, if you're born in this area, there's a roughly 4 percent chance that you will move up in economic status."[6]

In the 1950s and '60s, Jaren says, the Westside was a vibrant, mixed-income community. "You had doctors living next to dentists living next to sanitation workers and municipal employees," he says. "But it was for the wrong reason: the city was segregated. And back then, these neighborhoods were populated with about 50,000 folks, but today the population is closer to 15,000 or 16,000. That's a high volume of vacancy, but it translates to great capacity to retain current residents, bring back folks who were displaced, and welcome new residents."

April De Simone is a social-impact designer who cocreated a traveling exhibit, *Undesign the Redline*, that was shown in Atlanta, Boston, Chicago, New York, Washington, DC, and other cities. She notes that redlining's ongoing effects aren't just physical, but mental, which is just one reason they are so pernicious. Redlining functions as "a metaphor of division, of demarcation, an indelible line that says, 'I'm on this side and you're on that side.'"

Policies such as redlining and urban renewal reinforced a stratification system that put people on different levels, she says, creating the perception that some groups are less deserving of basic rights. This is a fundamental flaw in perception and a failure of love. April points to a kind of "redlined mental space" that calls for a "cognitive disruption" that will enable people to empathize with others in need.

"It's the most painful thing to watch the perpetuation of the hierarchy of human value," she says. "We need to be more empathetic toward housing and other conditions that will propel a just and inclusive lived experience for ALL human beings." And for that, she says, we need to codesign places that evoke humanism and simultaneously heal.

This is exactly where Quest shines, and where Nick feels called to work. Quest is providing not just socially equitable housing, but better access to healthcare, employment, financial services, and youth opportunities. Its model is working: Quest is Atlanta's largest nonprofit developer and owner of housing for people with below 30 percent AMI. Since its founding in 2000, the group has developed 369 units of affordable multifamily housing, eleven single-family homes, and three commercial community facilities.

Thanks to a holistic approach that promotes self-sufficiency, 90 percent of the organization's formerly unhoused clients do not return to homelessness. Quest's vision for the future includes investing $87 million in their Health & Housing models over the next three years, and construction of the Quest Nonprofit Center for Change, which will be a hub for the expansion of community development and economic-inclusion opportunities for the Westside community. It is slated for completion at the end of 2020.

Nick is only about halfway through his Rose Fellowship, but he's already partnered with numerous community development organizations to help bring an array of projects to fruition. On Joseph E. Lowery Boulevard, Quest developed a hundred units of affordable housing along with retail and office space. Quest Residences at Grove Park—forty units of affordable housing for people fifty-five and over—will also finish up in 2020.

Other projects still underway include Quest Commons West, an affordable, EarthCraft-certified[7] mixed-income building; an eight-unit building at 935 Hobson that will provide affordable housing for families with children in the Gideon Elementary School district; a number of single-family homes built in partnership with Habitat for Humanity; and Heritage Village at West Lake, the adaptive reuse of a 6-acre property into an affordable housing development with an urban farm.

The benefits to the community architects and residents are mutual. For example, this kind of multidisciplinary work has given Nick far more professional flexibility than his colleagues at traditional firms. Thinking about his career, "the mantra that I used was 'get free,'" he recalls. "Freedom to live the life I want to live, and freedom to experience the things I want to experience without any hesitation, without any barriers." At Quest, Nick has found that he has more autonomy as an architect and more ability to have a direct impact on the people he serves—that the personal liberation he experiences goes hand in hand with helping to liberate a community.

"I think it's important to communicate to people who are just coming out of school that there's another opportunity, another avenue," he says. "If you really want to create an impact, think about working for a community development organization, because that's where it starts. It gives you a seat at the ownership table. As architects, we get lauded for design and the way things look, but being in the decision-making chair, there's a lot more impact from that point, because you make the decisions; you say yes or no at the end of the day."

Recently, Nick bought a house in one of the neighborhoods Quest serves. "Now, when I talk about some of the work going on in the neighborhood, my neighbors see I have skin in the game, and whatever is going on here will impact me, too. That

nstruction of the Quest
nprofit Center for Change,
eph E. Lowery Boulevard

*HERO

Mural: *John Lewis*; Artist: Sean Schwab, Sweet Auburn Historic District

Home of Martin Luther King Jr. and Coretta Scott King, Sunset Avenue in the Vine City neighborhood

helps, as does building relationships with neighbors who can tell me the history of the community."

Through these relationships, Leonard Adams believed that he could make a difference "here in the beloved heart of the community," as he put it, when he launched the nonprofit twenty years ago. "I founded Quest in an effort to house homeless individuals who were living with a special condition of either mental illness or substance addiction," he says. "People were living on the streets and they needed a place to live, to gather themselves and, with support, be set on a rcnewed life's quest."

Starting with a single-family house, Quest has grown tremendously since then, but it still operates with the heart of a grassroots organization; team members are ready to provide whatever services are necessary to help clients gain and maintain self-sufficiency. Their attitude is one of empathy for the community members who need it most.

"I think it's important to communicate to people who are just coming out of school that there's another opportunity, another avenue. If you really want to create an impact, think about working for a community development organization, because that's where it starts." —Nick Forest

Nick credits his family for teaching him that kind of empathy, especially his grandparents and aunt, who were deeply involved in community work. "They never talked about what they did," he says. "They just saw what needed to be done, and they did the work. That's something I admired and I try to do as well. You see an issue; you just do something about it."

This pragmatic attitude, and his natural empathy, makes Nick especially effective. "I think in order to do this work, you have to love people," he says. "You have to understand that the issues people deal with and the positions they're in sometimes aren't of their own choice. So how then can we judge them for being where they are and say, 'Oh, they just need to get a job'? You have to see past their issues and mishaps to give them the second chance they need."

Leonard says, "Low-income housing or affordable housing is still a code name or dog whistle for low-income housing for poor and/or problematic black people, right? If you go to any affluent neighborhood and say, 'Hey, I want to bring affordable housing here,' alarm bells go off. That shouldn't be the dog whistle for poor black people coming to mess your neighborhood up." Which brings him back to love. "Dr. King's whole foundation was love," Leonard says. "You love that person, even if they're trying to hurt you. So yes, love is the most powerful single tool—it should be *the* antiracism tool, but it's not, because hate and fear are more superior."

Leonard continues. "If we don't get [the issue of] race right, we're going to be here fifty years from now, still doing the same thing," he says. "I think [these] policies that were written back in the day don't need to be fixed; they need to be thrown away. You can't fix what was designed as broken. We can't keep kicking the can and be in there tinkering in the engine when the whole engine was bad in the first place, right? Look, let's get rid of that engine. Let's go build a new engine!"

In addition to his work with Quest, Leonard serves on the board of HouseATL, a task force of civic leaders who have made a clear-eyed assessment of the barriers to affordable housing in Atlanta and created a comprehensive set of recommendations to overcome them.

Indeed, Quest is part of a wider team bringing systemic change to this city. For example, Ryan Gravel is a designer, builder, author, and serial entrepreneur whose 1999 Georgia Tech master's thesis formed the original vision for the 22-mile Atlanta BeltLine, a transportation and economic-development project that will connect neighborhoods throughout Atlanta. He recently worked with architects, urban planners, community builders, and arts enthusiasts at Atlanta City Studio to oversee the Atlanta City Design Project, a groundbreaking initiative that outlines a comprehensive vision of what Atlanta could and should look like in the future.

It's a bold and radical vision, an urban code based on love.

"The aftermath of the civil rights movement was supposed to be the Beloved Community," Ryan says, "which was not some utopian place but an actual place where people negotiated conflict and lived together in harmony. So this legacy is what sets Atlanta apart. We wanted to design a city that would be that Beloved Community, a city for everybody. We wanted to organize the decisions that are made about that future place around that inspiration."

The Atlanta City Design Project has been adopted into the City Charter of Atlanta, where it is used as the guiding principle for decisions about affordable housing, development, infrastructure, investment, zoning, services, and policy. The city has built its value system around the Beloved Community, and that happens neighborhood by neighborhood, initiative by initiative, storefront community meeting by town hall community meeting.

"We're going to neighborhood meetings and asking people what they want to see out of this design," Leonard says. "We want to be able to align [the community's input] with what Commissioner [Tim] Keane and his team at the Atlanta City Studio are doing. This is going to be a recipe for success for all of us. I hope that the Beloved Community will be a way to not displace current residents and to attract multitudes of demographics, races, and income levels in a collective neighborhood."

No one has built an ideal community—not yet. No one has ended racism and inequality—not yet. But these warriors for justice and equity, Rose Fellows among them, are on the path. They have been bold enough to resist despair in the face of massive social injustice, and instead to envision the world they want to see and then begin to build it. They are doing the work of the Beloved Community, this difficult and world-changing work, this necessary labor of love.

ulpture: *Homage to King*;
tist: Xavier Medina-Campeny

In 1960, Dr. Martin Luther King Jr. became a copastor of Ebenezer Baptist Church with his father, Rev. Martin Luther King Sr.

NEZER
PTIST
URCH

Thunder Valley, South Dakota

"I miss the landscape, I miss the work, I miss waking every morning to the meadowlarks and the sun cascading over the endless hills, I miss the peace, I miss the views. And mostly, I miss the people."

These are the words of Rose Fellow Kaziah Haviland, recalling her time working for the Thunder Valley Community Development Corporation (TVCDC) on the Pine Ridge Reservation in Porcupine, South Dakota. But she also remembers shedding many tears, especially during the first year of her fellowship.

"I was so overcome by the struggles I was witnessing," she says, "and I was almost blinded by the learning process I had to go through as I figured out my role outside a traditional architecture firm."

Though accurate information can be difficult to obtain, statistics routinely rank Pine Ridge as the "lowest and last" across multiple categories. According to the most recent US census data, the per capita income of residents of Oglala Lakota County (population 14,309) is just $9,334, with 41.5 percent of the population living in poverty.[1] Other sources point out that the Pine Ridge Indian Reservation has the lowest average life expectancy (66.8 years) in the US, and health statistics provided by the Oglala Sioux Tribe are nothing short of harrowing.[2]

Infant mortality rates on Pine Ridge are 300 percent higher than the American average, teen suicide is 150 percent higher, and tuberculosis rates are 800 percent higher. The school dropout rate is over 70 percent, half of adults over the age of forty have diabetes, and approximately 85 percent of Lakota families are affected by alcoholism.[3] Meanwhile, the dearth of good-quality, affordable homes on the reservation means most of the workforce must live elsewhere. For those who do stay, it is common for two or even three families to crowd together in a house built for a single family.

These were just a few of the conditions Kaziah encountered, leaving her unsure where to begin. Simultaneously, there were major cultural differences to negotiate. Kaziah and her husband, Greg Montgomery, also a licensed architect, moved from Austin, Texas, into a straw-bale home in Wakinyan Opha—"the place the thunder moves through"—in January 2016.

A Philadelphia native, Kaziah had never lived in a rural area. She had no familiarity with the enormous financial, legal, and political complexities of developing and building on tribal land. Her task was to learn everything at once and, with deep sensitivity to the culture and Lakota Sioux history, serve a community suffering from historical injustices.

Opposite: Chance Renville and son Ellis, residents, Thunder Valley Regenerative Community

"My first year was a rollercoaster of activity with a steep learning curve [and] a fast pace," she says. "But if I've learned one thing working at Thunder Valley CDC, it's no matter how hopeless a situation feels, right before the failing point, something will switch and the situation will correct with greater success than initially planned."

A powerful communal spirit, known in Lakota as *mitákuye oyás'iŋ*, infuses Lakota culture. Roughly translated as "we are all related," it acknowledges the deep interconnectedness of all things. "You hear that expression several times a day," Kaziah says. "Whether it's in a prayer or in conversation, it extends to everything. All things have worth and value. It's an entire code of culture." *Mitákuye oyás'iŋ* is so pervasive and foundational, in fact, that to try to speak about it as a concept unattached to lived experience is to do it a disservice. It is, simply, the way of life in Thunder Valley.

Tatewin Means, TVCDC's executive director and former legal counsel, says, "Everything we do in our spirituality is centered on giving back to the people. That connection is automatic. When you keep that spirituality, the focus and the people are the next step. So it's never [about] self-interest or self-motivation. It's always about the greater good."

Nick Tilsen agrees. A TVCDC founder and its executive director during Kaziah's fellowship, he says, "Embedded in our language, in our spirituality, in our ideology, in our worldview, is an acknowledgment that all things are made of energy, and these energies have an inter-relationship with each other. This is a totally different place to make decisions from. Which is why it's so important that indigenous languages don't get lost and the ceremonies don't get lost. It's our connection not only to the past, but to the future, and where we need to be going as a people."

Look anywhere and you can see *mitákuye oyás'iŋ* at work. At Thunder Valley CDC, each day begins with a ritual in which employees "circle up" to pray, burn sage, and share what's happening in their lives and what they're grateful for. Star Means, TVCDC's director of housing and a resident in TVCDC's Thunder Valley Apartments, says, "Starting off our morning with gratitude and prayer keeps the toxic workplace environment out. It's a beautiful place to be and a beautiful place to work."

Indeed, it was this Lakota spirit that led a group of young visionaries—Nick Tilsen and Thunder Valley resident Jerome LeBeaux among them—to create the TVCDC in 2007. "The CDC grew out of a cultural and spiritual movement of young people reconnecting to culture and identity, to a piece of us that was missing for so long," Nick says. "We found that [missing piece] through our language, through our ceremonies, through our prayers."

Jerome remembers a sweat lodge ceremony that marked a pivotal moment: "Our ancestors communicated to us that no one was holding us down except ourselves," he says. "They basically called us out and asked how long we were going to let other people decide the future for our children. And we came out of that lodge motivated to make a change. We didn't know what we were going to do yet, but we knew we needed housing, we needed jobs, we needed what you see [TVCDC] doing here."

Their ambitious, multipronged approach, called the Thunder Valley Regenerative Community, centers on key areas that together promote systemic change for the Lakota Nation and beyond: education, youth leadership, food sovereignty, preservation of the Lakota language, workforce development, social enterprise, and housing and homeownership.

"In places where there is deep poverty and generational economic problems, just building homes isn't going to solve anything," Kaziah says. "As Nick says, it has to be an entire 'ecosystem of opportunity.'"

Kaziah's primary area of focus was housing—and in the spirit of *mitákuye oyás'iŋ*, it wasn't just for people. Her first design project was a much-needed chicken coop. "And even that," she says, "was carefully planned to embody the culture of the Lakota."

With the help of an Enterprise Collaborative Action grant,[4] Kaziah worked with two Lakota artists who developed a design for the coop's solarium wall. Then, the community painted the wall and built the coop together. "There are the traditional [Lakota] colors of red, yellow, black, and white, which represent a unity of people all together," explains TVCDC team member and traditional quillworker Mary LeBeau. "And the circle represents that there's no beginning, there's no end, nobody above, nobody under—we're all going in one direction."

Kaziah's main fellowship project, however, was implementing a master plan for Pine Ridge, a 34-acre mixed-use development. Andy Iron Shell, a member of the Cherokee Nation who was raised in Thunder Valley, recalls that residents rejected the initial plan to fill the parcel with housing stock. "The community came back and said, 'No, that's not really what we want,'" Andy says. "They wanted things to do, a school, maybe a store. And then the first layout looked very linear—all parallel streets, very American-pie-looking. So we went back to the drawing board for another eighteen months, and now [the design] is much more culturally appropriate. There's a lot more circles, and the houses are laid out in a horseshoe shape that shows the hierarchy of how we used to camp in the tipi days. . . . Back then there was a sense of shared resources, shared parenting, really a sense of community."

The new scheme fulfilled the community's wishes to create a physical world that reflects their spiritual values. It called for twenty-one single-family homes, a twelve-unit apartment building, and a community center with a guest house. The buildings were to be both beautiful and sustainable, able to withstand the climatic extremes of South Dakota, where temperatures can reach -30 degrees Fahrenheit in winter and 120 degrees in summer, and winds can gust to 120 mph.

To involve the community further and keep costs down, the shell of the homes would be built by commercial contractors, while the interior and finish-out work would be supplemented by TVCDC's Workforce Development Program and Self-Help Program participants. Native-owned Thikaga Construction, born out of the workforce development program, took over the commercial contracts for framing the final fourteen homes. This provided participants with steady work and income after graduating from the program and ensured the homes would be built by community members. Eighteen homes would sell for market rate, while the remaining homes would employ subsidies and self-help sweat-equity hours to lower the cost of the mortgages. The apartment building would also offer a mix of market-rate and low-income units.

This model was a significant step up. Housing on Native American reservations tends to be poorly planned, designed, and constructed. What the community needed

Kaziah Haviland, Rose Fellow, 2016–2018

DELTA
VENT SA
Haugen

DELTA

Tatewin Means, Executive Director, Thunder Valley CDC

Nick Tilsen, Founder, Thunder Valley CDC

was homes spacious enough to accommodate large families, strong enough to last at least four generations, and affordable enough for a population that suffers from job insecurity, unemployment, and poor credit.

The reality, however, is that 85 percent of the homes in Pine Ridge are trailers—flimsy, inefficient structures that immediately depreciate in value, undermining any chance of building equity and passing on generational wealth. This outcome reflects a stunning mismatch between the American banking system and the needs of people on the reservation: lenders won't finance site-built homes on a reservation because they can't foreclose on the land.

For Kaziah, it was a frustrating lesson on the financial barriers to providing good-quality housing on tribal land. "Building on the reservation is estimated to be anywhere between 15 and 20 percent more expensive because of the remote location and the associated liability," she says. "We also pay a 4 percent TERO (Tribal Employment Rights Ordinance) tax and a 1 percent environmental tax, tacking an additional 5 percent onto the cost of building. This leaves us at a minimum 20–25 percent higher cost than building in an urban setting, right off the bat."

A rural area lacks the economies of scale found in more-populated regions. There is no existing infrastructure to tap into, and equipment and materials have to be hauled in from a distance. The weather also plays a role. One year, construction was delayed because the water and sewer had not yet been installed due to a late thaw and frozen ground.

"There were no systems in place that took into account the realities of building where we were building," Kaziah says. Yet she speaks highly of the South Dakota Housing Development Authority, because "they really tried to make changes to make the loan programs work for us."

"In places where there is deep poverty and generational economic problems, just building homes isn't going to solve anything. As Nick says, it has to be an entire 'ecosystem of opportunity.'"
—Kaziah Haviland

Construction delays and budget shortfalls weren't the only problems hampering the progress. "Another challenge was the constant shifting of our project team," Kaziah recalls. "At one point we had three different project managers and two different construction managers all within one year." The team faced another major challenge when over half of the leadership staff left for five months to join the protest at Standing Rock.

"Nick was hard to reach during this time," Kaziah says. "He relied on me and the other program managers to step up and start making some of the hard decisions. I am grateful I had others to lean on." And, Thunder Valley's communal vision provided a true north. "What made it all work was that though Nick could articulate the vision like no one else, it wasn't only his vision; it was a shared vision."

She also took solace from the place itself. "Whenever the emotional weight or work-related obstacles left me feeling defeated, I climbed the hill that overlooks the development and saw it rising up little by little and I was inspired to keep pushing."

Fortunately, organizations such as TVCDC are challenging the existing models and, if they need to, rewriting the rules. TVCDC broke ground on phase 1 in September

ome LeBeaux, Cultural Coordinator, Thunder Valley CDC

Thunder Valley Regenerative Community, Porcupine, SD. Developer: Thunder Valley CDC; Architect: BNIM and Pyatt Studio

2016, while half the team was still in Standing Rock. Construction on the first seven of the twenty-one single-family homes began the following month. The team continued to apply for funding sources and handled every hurdle as it arose, from labor shortages to securing last-minute waivers to cover budget deficits. Kaziah can now look back on it all with a smile.

"We were in constant hot water—we always needed cash and needed it now," she says. "But through the hard work of a united team, we were able to make so much happen."

Nick never lost hope. "I was always taught that when something's hard, it's for a reason," he says. "Whenever there's hardship, there's a great reward, because you're meeting the Creator halfway. You're putting your blood, sweat, and tears into something. That makes it *wakan*—that makes it sacred."

Thunder Valley Apartments, a beautiful two-story building, features sustainable design elements such as power-saving LED lights and water-saving sinks, faucets, toilets, and showers. Half of the apartments are designated for people who earn 50–60 percent of the area median income (AMI).

"When we opened applications for the apartment building, I got to work about 7:30 in the morning, and there were literally sixty people waiting on the deck to get in for the applications," says Star Means. Now fully occupied, Thunder Valley Apartments offers three floor plans and embodies the vision of regenerative community.

The 1,200-square-foot community house, meanwhile, was built with a large, double-height open space for community events, family gatherings, and classes. A local artist advisory council convened by TVCDC helped design the community house to ensure that culture and spirituality were adequately expressed.

In designing this space—the only community facility in the area—the team asked themselves, What does modern Lakota architecture look like? Community members rejected the first sketch featuring a pitched roof. The new scheme features a butterfly roof and clerestory windows that open the interior to the sky—a reinterpretation of the tipi. "The first thing people do when they walk into the space is look up," Kaziah says. "Similar to the tipi, there is a low, humble entry, and you come into a large shared space and your eye is drawn to the sky."

An adjacent 3,800 square feet contains several bunk rooms, two kitchens, a lobby, and bathrooms. The "green spine" portion of the overall project features a basketball court, skateboard park, playground, grill pits, horseshoe pits, public restroom pavilion, and landscaped space, including an herb garden.

The Cooper Hewitt, Smithsonian Design Museum in New York City selected this project for inclusion in its 2016–2017 show *By the People: Designing a Better America*. But the ultimate proof of its success is on the ground. With phase 1 nearing completion, the development is what the community calls a "show-me place," proving what is possible on the reservation. Designed as a place of healing for generations to come, it is the result of hundreds of hours of community engagement and a belief that the answers come from within the community, not from outside agendas. Its success is also the result of understanding existing systems and doing whatever it takes to work against—or around—them.

Design based on spiritual belief may seem unusual, but as Nick observes, "Sometimes we have to get people to think differently, behave differently, because the status quo

Thikaga Construction,
Thunder Valley Regenerative
Community

THUNDER VALLEY
L35E LSL RIM BOARD PLUS
1-1/4 CAT
PR-L280
L35E LSL RIM BOARD PLUS

Thunder Valley Climate Change Resilient Housing, Porcupine, SD. Developer: Thunder Valley CDC; Architect: Pyatt Studio

hasn't served the majority of the people. We are not human beings on a spiritual journey; we are spiritual beings on a human journey. The human journey's an opportunity to leave our imprint on this world. What kind of imprint do we want to leave?"

As for Kaziah, Thunder Valley's imprint is profound. "I learned a lot about being an architect and what I want to do, and I left with an incredibly diverse skill set—everything from event planning to graphic design to balancing a budget to writing reports and funding applications," she says. "Thunder Valley was so beautiful, and such a unique place. We will forever feel lucky to have lived there."

It's clear how deeply she misses Thunder Valley—and how firmly the community embraced Kaziah and Greg and their daughter, Matilda, who was born in 2018. "Matilda's gonna forever be attached to this place!" says Tatewin proudly. "When she gets older and says, 'Mom and Dad, I'm going back to the rez!,' it's because she was born here."

After her fellowship ended, Kaziah worked remotely with TVCDC to write their design guidelines, and Greg started working for former Rose Fellowship host organization Cathedral Square, which provides affordable senior housing in Burlington, Vermont. Greg and Kaziah have also launched their own design firm, Osso Studio.

The house they left in Thunder Valley is now a Lakota immersion Montessori school. With only 3 percent of the population fluent in Lakota, the community's dream is to build a Lakota immersion middle school and high school, because embedded in their language is the spirit of *wakinyan opha*, the place the thunder moves through, and the beloved community who live on its land.

DELTA

Los Angeles, California

When Theresa Hwang came to the Skid Row Housing Trust to interview for the Rose Fellowship, she walked around the chaotic neighborhood and thought, "Can I do this?"

A second-generation Korean American, Theresa had spent her entire life in the Northeast. She would be leaving behind friends and family and starting over in a wholly unfamiliar city. And the job would be, to say the least, enormous.

"I knew I would be working with poor communities," she says, "but the issues in the neighborhood and the scale of the shortage of housing felt like problems so much bigger than me that I worried I wouldn't have anything to contribute or any ability to make an impact when I first arrived."

Home to over 10,000 residents, one-third of whom live in shelters or outside in tents and on the streets, Skid Row has a long-standing reputation as one of America's grimmest neighborhoods.[1] A dearth of public toilets and trash cans makes for deplorable and often-unsafe conditions. Outbreaks of hepatitis A, tuberculosis, and other infectious illnesses are common. And although unhoused people anywhere are at greater risk of experiencing violence, poor health, and substance abuse, Skid Row has become an emblem of the desperation faced by the homeless in Los Angeles and nationally.

That this place exists in one of the world's most prosperous nations, nestled in the heart of one of its largest and most glamorous cities, only underscores the tragedy of Skid Row. A local artist who runs an arts collaborative says that Skid Row is "the predictable result of a profoundly sick society," one that forces large numbers of people—mostly people of color, many women and children—to live in the violence of homelessness and poverty.

After nine years of working closely with residents and housing advocates in Skid Row, Theresa has gained a view of the neighborhood that runs much deeper than the dominant narrative. Despite the work yet to be done to address the conditions that gave rise to Skid Row, she has been deeply inspired by the strength, self-determination, and courage it takes to survive here. "I know I was meant to come here," says Theresa. "And I'm just thankful to have been embraced by this community."

Skid Row has long been a place where poor people have lived and congregated. When the transcontinental railroad was completed in 1875, Los Angeles was the end of the line. By the 1880s, with transient or unemployed people riding the train to warmer climates, the area around the rail terminal was called Hobo Corner, characterized by bars and single-room occupancy (SRO) hotels. For a while, city officials did nothing to help this area, or to discourage it. But by 1906, LA residents began to complain, and the

Skid Row
CITY LIMIT
POP Too Many
ELEV 2008

A meal from the Los Angeles Catholic Worker Hospitality Kitchen, "Hippie Kitchen," East 6th Street

NO TRESPASSING
NO LODGING/ BLOCKING SIDEWALKS
419
419
DO NOT BLOCK

NO TRESPASSING
NO LODGING/ BLOCKING SIDEWALKS
421
Sample

city made an effort to get people off the street. Streetlights were installed and police started making arrests for drunkenness and loitering. By the 1920s the community was moved east to the area we now know as Skid Row.

Its population increased during the Great Depression and again in the 1960s. By the mid-1980s, a number of factors compounded to make homelessness a systemic reality not just in Los Angeles but across the United States. In the 1970s and 1980s, the economy shifted from manufacturing jobs to service industry jobs, with salaries so low that even working families were living below the poverty line. At the same time, nearly five million affordable-housing units were lost to the private sector, and the US government defunded public housing.[2]

Other social policies contributed, too. "Deinstitutionalization" was the plan to empty the asylums treating and housing mentally disabled individuals. In California alone, the population in psychiatric institutions dropped from over half a million to just over 100,000, and because of the lack of alternative treatment systems, a huge number of these patients ended up on the street. Welfare and federal programs to help the poor were so drastically reduced that by the early 1990s, 20 percent of America's children lived in poverty.[3]

Meanwhile, the introduction of crack cocaine in the 1980s turned drug use into a truly terrifying social issue. Crack was cheap, plentiful, and hideously addictive and wreaked havoc on lives and communities. In addition, the rising cost of healthcare and health insurance meant that many people with medical problems had no access to affordable healthcare. By the early 1990s, 2.7 million people in Los Angeles County lacked health insurance. People often faced a choice between paying for healthcare or housing, and as a result many people found themselves homeless.[4]

In a series of federally funded revitalization efforts in the 1960s and 1970s, many cities created redevelopment plans that displaced poor people from centrally located neighborhoods. In an unlikely alignment between LA's city planners and advocates for the poor, however, a plan was created that included a "policy of containment" in which the fifty-block area of Skid Row would be set aside as a neighborhood serving the poor. It was adopted by the Los Angeles City Council in 1976.[5]

Considered progressive compared to how other American cities were treating their homeless residents at the time, the zone protected the rights of poor people to live in a downtown neighborhood, but it also neglected to provide them with basic city services. The containment plan advocated some fairly radical ideas, including pushing all the missions, shelters, charities, and other homeless services into the newly drawn borders of Skid Row, and the inclusion of public restrooms, benches, and open spaces. These "inducements" were intended to encourage the poor population to remain within their zone.[6]

To dissuade homeless people from expanding their territory, officials used harsh urban design elements such as prison-style lighting on Skid Row's bordering streets. Meanwhile, police officers were more likely to leave people alone if they stayed within the borders of the containment zone, and the Los Angeles Redevelopment Agency left the area largely intact. It would also eventually form the SRO Housing Trust, charged with protecting and maintaining low-income housing in Skid Row. And so, over the course of just a few years, Skid Row became the place to go if you were homeless in Los Angeles.[7]

Volunteer barbershop,
Gladys Park

Though many people imagine it to be a primarily transient neighborhood, for its residents, Skid Row is a community. Skid Row is home.

During a recent visit with Theresa, I met Suzette Shaw, a resident of Skid Row. As Suzette recounted her story over lunch, her arrival here seemed both impossible and inevitable. Born in 1963 in Zuma, Arizona, Suzette moved to California, where she had a successful career in Silicon Valley and later owned a business. She also suffered from discrimination as an unmarried African American woman and frequent job changes.

Even while employed, making ends meet in the Bay Area became increasingly difficult. To find housing that was affordable, Suzette had to endure long commutes to work. When that became financially unsustainable, she began staying on friends' and relatives' couches, all of which left her increasingly desperate. She went back home to her family in Zuma, where she was met with hostility. The impact of abuse she suffered as a child reasserted itself, and her life became unhinged. The downward spiral ultimately took her to Skid Row in December 2012.

Suzette now lives in the New Genesis Apartments, a project of the Skid Row Housing Trust (known as the Trust), a permanent supportive housing nonprofit that provides residents with a variety of services such as case management, mental health services, life skills training, and support groups. New Genesis has an on-site health clinic and community spaces, including a kitchen, lounge, and courtyard gardens. A neighborhood leader and advocate for the poor, Suzette serves on boards and speaks from hard-won experience about the need for healthcare and housing.

"People think blessings are positive," Suzette says, "but blessings are born of pain. If we are willing to go through the pain, the triumph is on the other side. Skid Row found me. This is where I am supposed to be."

Trained as an architect, Theresa has long been a crusader for social justice and an advocate for community-based arts. Before she moved to Los Angeles, she received her master's degree in architecture but left the field to work with an Asian American arts coalition in Boston. She wanted to deploy her design skills for social justice.

As a Rose Fellow, Theresa was in the unique position of being a staff designer with the housing development and part of the asset management team at Skid Row Housing Trust. This enabled her to further not only the Trust's commitment to designing *for* residents, but to designing *with* residents. Theresa recognized that residents not only have opinions about their neighborhood, but as the local experts they have solutions. She engaged residents at many of the Trust's properties to ask: "What works? What doesn't? What's most important? How does this space make you feel? And how does this space work best?"

Theresa spent a year going to meetings in the neighborhood, listening to the perspectives of residents, as well as other nonprofit service providers and advocates, and asking, "How can I support your efforts?" She documented those insights in order to incorporate them proactively into the design process of future projects—including one of her favorite buildings.

Working part-time with Michael Maltzan Architecture, Theresa used the input she gained from residents to influence the design of the Star Apartments, a gorgeous, cantilevered building that used an existing one story commercial structure as a base

zette Shaw, resident and
tivist, Skid Row

Theresa Hwang, Rose Fellow, 2009-2012, and Michael Maltzan, Principal,
Michael Malzan Architecture

to hold 102 prefabricated modular apartments. The former roof of the commercial structure provides a podium for outdoor recreation, a community garden, offices, a health-and-wellness center, community kitchen, and art rooms.

The Skid Row Housing Trust and SRO Housing have created or preserved 3,500 units of affordable housing, including Suzette's home. Much of the work was done with health and human services integrated into the programming. Mike Alvidrez, former executive director of the Trust, says their approach has evolved. In the early days, the Trust focused on acquisition and rehabilitation and tried to buy as many buildings as they could while the policy and financial environment allowed it. SRO apartments provided housing but did not have space for supportive services. And many of those early buildings contained dark, small rooms, with bathrooms located down unlit corridors.

While these apartments provided shelter, they did not adequately help people remake their lives. The Trust came to the conclusion that utilitarian housing was not enough to provide a formerly homeless person with the resources to stay stably housed. What they needed to create was high-quality housing with supportive services.

"The saying that 'home is where your heart is' is a reminder that we all carry our notion of home, of belonging and identity, with us wherever we go. Regardless of housing status, each individual still has the right to live a full life, and to be without a permanent place to live should not mean that we lose our identity, or our souls." —Theresa Hwang

In 2016, 75 percent of Los Angeles voters supported Measure H and Proposition HHH, which together provided $3.5 billion in sales tax revenue and a $1.2 billion bond to finance 10,000 units of affordable housing with on-site services for homeless residents who had disabling conditions. Enterprise Community Partners was involved in the planning that led to the Los Angeles City and County homeless initiatives, and then helped get Measure H and Proposition HHH passed through voter outreach and public-awareness efforts.[8]

The adoption of these measures is a clear indication that Los Angeles residents want to provide housing for the homeless population. That said, resident groups often protest the introduction of such projects in their own neighborhoods. The Trust has learned that great design is the best tool to combat this not-in-my-backyard mentality.

"Beauty cracks open the door," Mike says. "If it's a good building, then people feel good about it." The building becomes part of the urban fabric, and rather than protesting the residents, neighbors focus on the valuable addition to the neighborhood.

The strategy works: the Trust has now developed twenty-six supportive-housing buildings in Los Angeles County, with three more under construction.[9] They have an astonishing 90 percent success rate in keeping people housed during that critical first year after they're off the streets.

Part of the reason is that the team shifted their focus from individual buildings to the entire neighborhood. Theresa joined with Suzette, who was an active Skid Row advocate, and sixteen other volunteer Resident Block Leaders to collaborate on Our Skid Row, an initiative to analyze the needs in the neighborhood and brainstorm solutions. They got input from nearly 400 residents and held fifteen community meetings. "Skid Row is such an organized group—they know what they want," Theresa says. "And it was never about

Above and opposite: Star Apartments, Los Angeles. Developer: Skid Row Housing Trust; Architect: Michael Maltzan Architecture

charity or handouts. This was the people, the residents, who supported every single step and helped lead the process and build [their own] power. There was a feeling of, 'We are in it together,' which is why we called it Our Skid Row."

Advocate Charles Porter, who has worked in Skid Row with the United Coalition East Prevention Project for nineteen years, agrees. "This is a strong and beautiful place to be," he says. "People are not helpless, but rather they are starved for resources."

Our Skid Row invested in the public space with amenities serving everyone, including the unhoused. For example, ReFresh Spot fills a long-standing community need by providing twenty-four-hour access to restrooms, showers, and laundry facilities. This initiative highlights that wellness is a clear priority, and is reinforced by the prevalence of farmers markets, art events, and cultural activities in the area. Charles calls this *La Cultura Cura*, or the notion that cultural identity is at the core of a larger message of empowerment and healing.

"The saying that 'home is where your heart is' is a reminder that we all carry our notion of home, of belonging and identity, with us wherever we go," Theresa says. "Regardless of housing status, each individual still has the right to live a full life, and to be without a permanent place to live should not mean that we lose our identity, or our souls."

For this reason, she doesn't like to use the word "homeless." In her estimation, the term lumps the plight of individuals and families into an unnuanced societal problem. Further, the notion of home is so closely tied to our individual identity that to be without a home can be perceived as being faceless, or even soulless.

"It's not like they don't have a sense of being or community," Theresa says. "They're just unhoused."

Theresa remains at the forefront of efforts to design safe, just, and vibrant neighborhoods based on community engagement. "Anytime people are effectively mobilizing a collective group, it's just beautiful," she says.

It is fair to say that Skid Row not only changed the trajectory of her career but sparked profound inner shifts as well. Deeply inspired by the courage she witnessed there, Theresa says she connected with residents on a personal level and, in the process, fell in love with the community. That took courage and vulnerability on her part, and it took showing up as her full, authentic self.

"I needed to be there as Theresa and not just a staff person," she says. "I learned that someone who's living on Skid Row, their fulfillment and their sense of freedom, is actually intimately tied up with my sense of freedom. And really understanding that on a personal level was meaningful and important for me to experience."

When that happens—when we engage in work that dissolves the boundaries between people—we don't have to accept that millions of members of our society live outdoors or move from shelter to shelter. We don't have to accept a housing policy that allows this condition to exist.

Theresa's experience illustrates that designers and developers have tools to affect not only the policies and financial systems that create affordable housing, but the environments that afford every person the dignity and stability they deserve. What can we offer? We can design spaces that are "so livable, so welcoming," Theresa says, "that it's home. Just home."

eresa Hwang, marching in
Skid Row "Walk the Talk"
rade, with her daughter and
yk Makhmuryan, Studio 526

Walter Fears, Los Angeles Poverty Department (LAPD), marching in the Skid Row "Walk the Talk" Parade

Yakima, Washington

"Think of this the next time you're in the grocery store," says Nate Poel, Rose Fellow in Yakima Valley. "Even in our mechanized age, every scrap of produce on the shelf was harvested by a human hand. As a kid from the land of combines, that still blows my mind."

Nate was raised in northeastern Iowa, land of big agriculture and small communities steeped in Dutch heritage and Calvinism. A person of deep faith and empathy, Nate had long been interested in issues of social justice. When immigrants who had traveled from Honduras to the US and back again spoke about their experiences at one of his college classes, Nate was profoundly moved.

"It was some of the most powerful storytelling I've ever heard," he says, and it got him thinking. "If we're going to be debating immigration in the United States," he recalls telling a classmate, "at a minimum we need to know who it is we're talking about."

Nate studied abroad during his senior year of college, traveling from Honduras to Guatemala to Mexico City, and then across the border into Arizona, where he spent two weeks with No Más Muertes, a group providing humanitarian aid in the desert. The next week he started architecture school at the University of Oregon, and the spring before he graduated, he discovered the Rose Fellowship post in the Yakima Valley, which focused on seasonal farmworker housing. "And that right there, that was the connection," Nate says. "That was the link between my interests in the migrant experience, architecture, and social justice, and I knew that is where I wanted to be."

In contrast to his home state, where government-subsidized fields of corn and soybeans stretched out as far as the eye could see, the agriculture of the Yakima Valley, where Nate lives with his wife, Anna, is mostly fresh produce. With an average 300 days of sunshine per year and very little rain, melting snowpack from the Cascade Mountains allows more than forty commercial crops to grow in the valley. It's known for its abundant apples, hops, asparagus, cherries, grapes, and watermelon. A full 70 percent of the apples in America, and 20 percent of the hops in the world, are grown in the Yakima Valley. And all the crops are picked by hand.

However, a pattern has been in play since the early twentieth century, when settlers first established orchards here. To harvest their crops, farm owners, called growers—nearly all of Anglo descent—rely on seasonal workers, called pickers, most of whom travel from Mexico each year. The number of permanent residents in Yakima County is about 250,000.[1] But each year during picking season, the population swells by as many as 66,000 as workers take up residence.

Nathan Poel, Rose Fellow, 2012–2014

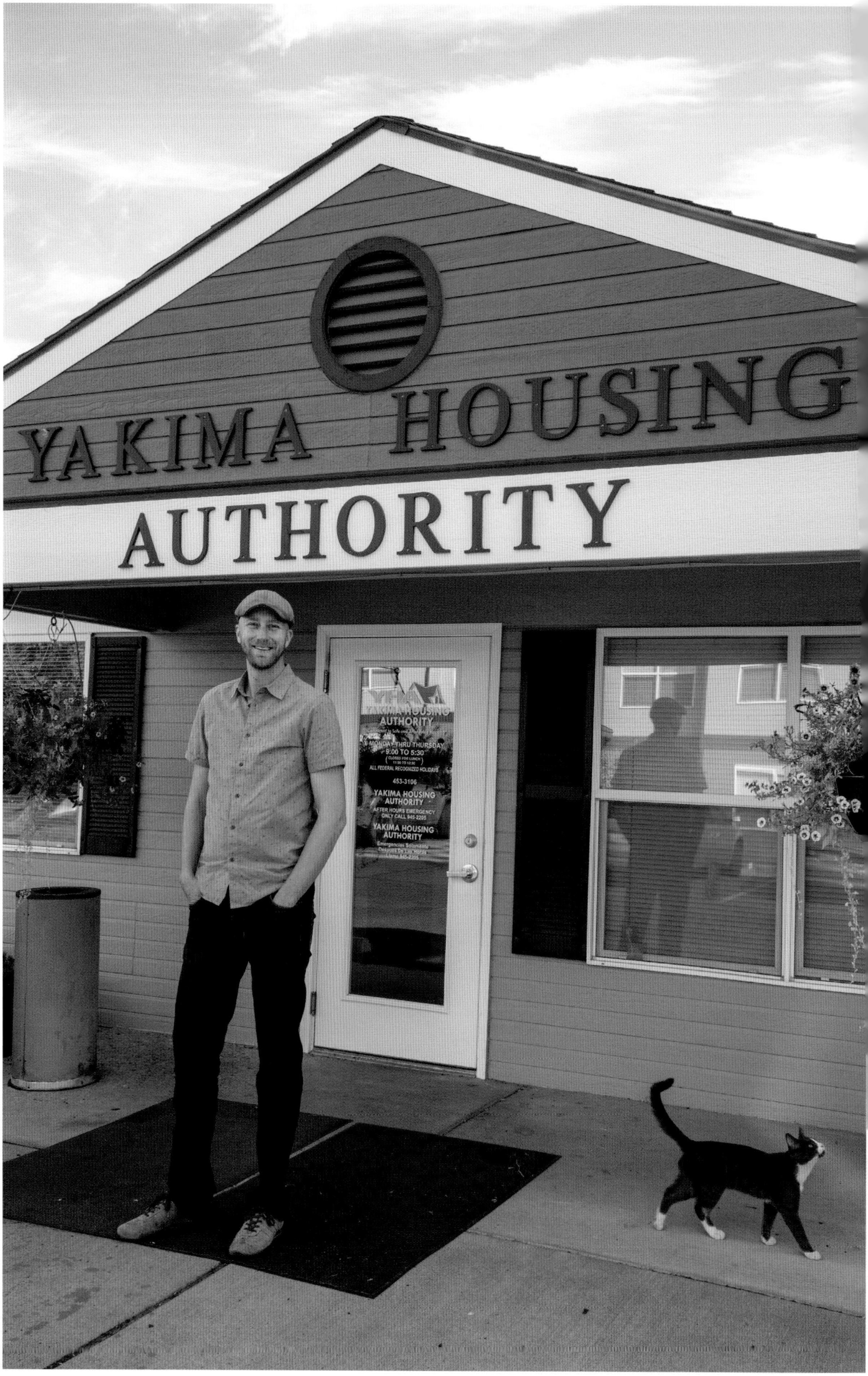

And although the migrant labor force has recently declined somewhat due to stricter immigration laws, tighter border security, and increasing opportunity at home, the demand for seasonal workers is vast. "I tell people the work is temporary," Nate says, "but the need is permanent. As long as there's agriculture in this valley, we will need seasonal workers coming in to help with the crops."

While they're doing the hard work of harvesting the nation's produce, every one of those workers will need the same services and support that every other person needs: housing, healthcare, education, job training, and community. The H-2A visa program, which allows nonimmigrant agricultural workers to be in the US for up to ten months, provides something of a safety net, since H-2A employers are required to provide workers with housing, transportation, and guaranteed wages.

But the quality of housing varies widely, and without access to health insurance, worker's compensation, adequate training, and other benefits, the seasonal worker population is at a disadvantage.

Indeed, the National Center for Farmworker Health attests that "agricultural workers represent some of the most economically disadvantaged people in the US." The disadvantages are not only economic, of course. Compared to the general population, seasonal farmworkers are at greater risk of workplace injury, poor overall health, isolation, instability, and substandard living and working conditions.[2] Reports of widespread sexual violence in the fields are well documented,[3] and any number of factors—fear, language and cultural barriers, lack of transportation, or simply not knowing how or where to find help in an unfamiliar place—make accessing services all the more difficult. Undocumented workers are at even greater risk, as the constant fear of deportation silences many.

"I was raised by a church community that taught us to love our neighbor," Nate says. "I can't think of one exception to this rule. 'Love your neighbor' does not stop at the border, or at a language barrier. It is not ascribed along with legal status or lawfulness. 'Love your neighbor' is fundamental. It lies at the very center of how we define ourselves as a people. In a globally connected society, your neighbor can be almost anyone, but it always includes the people you interact with, either by choice or by circumstance."

During his Rose Fellowship, Nate focused primarily on designing safe, affordable housing for migrant farmworkers. Learning from experts—people who have experienced farmwork firsthand—has been critical to his ability to do that well.

It was through a service project with Catholic Charities Housing Services (CCHS), which owns and manages housing throughout the Yakima Valley, that he met Sandra Aguilar, a CCHS resident services coordinator who grew up working as a picker. She exemplifies the challenges of the migrant farmworker experience.

Every year, Sandra, her parents, and four siblings traveled from Jalisco in west-central Mexico to California, Oregon, and Washington, following the harvests and working in each field for two to three weeks at a time. She remembers spending every June in Yakima picking cherries. Sandra's family had a pickup truck with a trailer that they lived in. She felt isolated, not remaining anywhere long enough to build friendships with other children. Her friends were her siblings.

Efrain Galvan, farm worker,
McIlrath Farms, Tieton, WA

Farmworker housing, circa 1930

Sandra Aguilar, Resident Services Coordinator, Catholic Charities Housing Services

For Sandra, cancer was part of her family's daily life since her father was diagnosed in 1989 at age forty-nine. She believes his cancer was related to pesticide exposure, and recalls how small aircraft dumped pesticides from the sky while workers were picking. Pesticides were "caked on" the fruits they picked, causing "burning in [my] esophagus and belly," she says. Her father died of cancer in 2005.

Sandra picked every year until the age of nineteen, when, against her father's wishes, she signed up for Job Corps training in computer programming. She went on to earn a master's degree in clinical psychotherapy. Sandra has a full life of community involvement, writing and performing music, and working at CCHS, where, as resident services program manager, she oversees staff delivering an array of services, including afterschool programs. Sandra works with many migrant farmworkers and elders who have experienced trauma.

Now with CCHS for over a decade, Sandra hopes her efforts will spark long-lasting change. "In the work that I do, I want [people] to understand and see how we need to work toward making systemic change happen through establishing pathways and systems of equity and inclusion that will dismantle the current system to make it better for all of us," she says. "We're graduating more students from high school and college each year and providing more opportunities to them. I predict they will naturally work toward changing a system that needs changing in order to be fair and equitable to all people."

Change may come easier to Washington State than to other places. A decade ago, the affordable-housing shortage forced large numbers of the state's migrant farmworkers to live in illegal campsites in wooded areas. These makeshift camps spawned a host of problems—inadequate latrines, poor sanitation, open campfires—and the state responded with emergency housing that Nate describes as "the first iteration of organized seasonal farm housing." Legally defined as "temporary worker housing," seasonal farmworker housing is a hybrid model, a combination of transient housing (like a hotel) and permanent housing (like an apartment).

The first example was the Pangborn Cherry Harvest Camp, which opened in 2004 and ran for five years. Consisting of fifty 14-by-20-foot repurposed army tents that could house up to seven workers at minimal cost ($3 per person per night or $10 per family), Pangborn provided basic shelter with shared kitchens and bathrooms.

Since then, many advances have been made—some due in part to Nate's work at the Office of Rural and Farmworker Housing (ORFH), where he developed farmworker housing in five rural communities throughout Central Washington, including in Granger, Prosser, Sunnyside, Cashmere, and Mattawa.

The hybrid nature of temporary worker housing presents unique challenges for designers, and Nate works constantly to improve the model to meet the needs of this specific community. One pressing issue community members brought to Nate was the need for outside storage space. Without it, workers must take their soiled and pesticide-contaminated clothing into the places where they eat and sleep. In response, the design Nate and his team worked on for Yakima Housing Authority's Cosecha Court, which provides housing for up to seventy-six seasonal workers, includes secure outdoor storage areas where workers could place their boots and work clothes, leaving the living spaces free of contaminants.

Above and opposite: Cosecha Court II, Granger, WA. Developer: Yakima Housing Authority; Architect: SMR Architects

A3

Nate also learned that well-designed temporary housing means not just a sufficient number of showers, beds, ovens, refrigerators, and laundry facilities, but also areas that can accommodate many people at once. Again in response to resident feedback, kitchen burners were reconfigured to accommodate multiple cooks. The houses were also equipped with Wi-Fi and air-conditioning, things many people take for granted but that are not typically included in housing designated for temporary use. Wi-Fi is particularly appreciated, since it allows migrant workers to stay in touch with family at home.

In addition, Cosecha Court includes common areas where people can gather to watch sports and "be loud and rowdy together," Nate says, which then ensures that "residential areas are places where people can be quiet." Similarly, a separate television area lets people watch TV without disrupting the rest of the house. These simple touches are what make a house feel like a home for residents, whether they stay a few weeks or several months. Phase II of Cosecha Court, which will include two residential buildings and a new community center, is slated to begin in February 2020.

Given his passion for social justice and deep faith, perhaps it's inevitable that Nate eventually brings up the idea of love as a tool for urban design. "This is why we're here," he says. "This is what the Rose Fellowship is all about. It's about trying to create the physical places, and the processes with which we make these physical places, in a way that cares about the other and creates a welcoming space for someone we have no other reason to love than the fact that they're there and they are human. And that's enough. You can love someone just for that."

"The initial idea [behind the Rose Fellowship] was that affordable housing needed more rigorous design and that designers, if they're trained well, make good developers. The fellowship exists to meld those two worlds more seamlessly." —Nate Poel

Nate met Amanda Ontiveros through Yakima Maker Space, a nonprofit community creative hub he cofounded while a Rose Fellow. Amanda was born in Washington State but calls herself Mexican. Her primary language is Spanish, and she grew up in a family of pickers, as did her husband and his family. By the age of seventeen, Amanda was pregnant and living back and forth between Yakima and Tieton, about 20 miles away in apple country. She now has four children ages seventeen to twenty-three. None of them have ever picked fruit, and they never will. When her youngest was seven, Amanda enrolled at Yakima Valley College. She began by studying business but decided to follow her passion and switched to art, ultimately graduating from Central Washington University with a BFA in studio art. "It feels good doing what I want," she says. "What I love."

The Maker Space provides tools, 3-D printers, sewing machines, studio space, and, most important, a sense of community and connection. Amanda discovered the Maker Space two years after it opened, and now visits "every chance I get." She works in paint, ceramics, jewelry, printmaking, and other crafts and has taught workshops in pottery, woodworking, and jewelry design.

"Amanda is a good example of the second generation of what's happening in the Hispanic community in Yakima," Nate says. She's active in the community and has built

anda Ontiveros, artist,
ima Maker Space

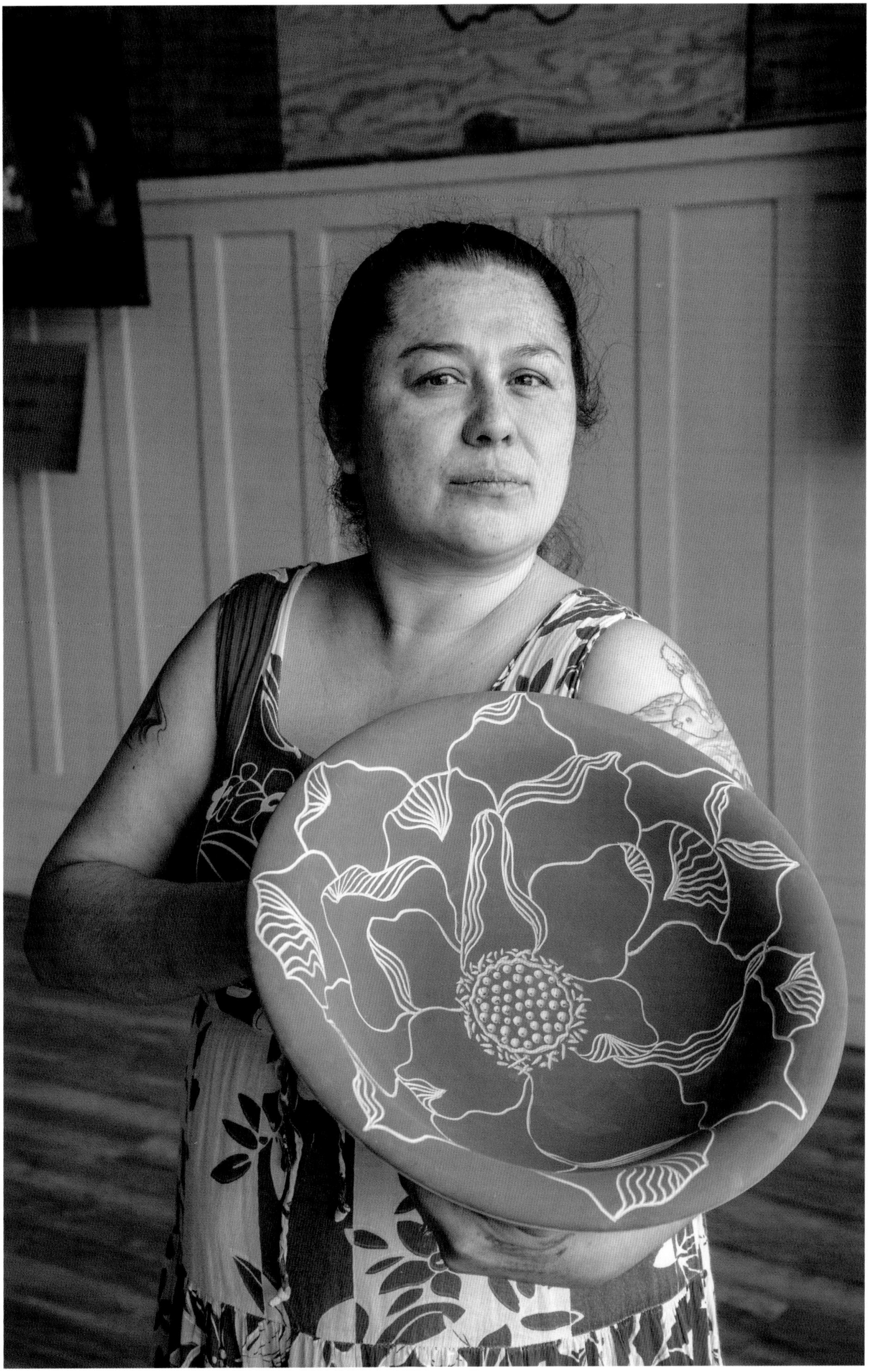

maker space
Please use
our YMS door
16 S. 1st Street
COLLABORATE
EDUCATE
CREATE
yms
3D PRINTING
VINYL CUTTING
CNC
POTTERY
ARDUINO
Yakima

a new life for herself and her children. She made the mugs for the coffee shop next door, and the plates for a restaurant down the street. This is locally sourced talent at its best.

When his Rose Fellowship concluded in 2014, Nate and Anna decided to stay in Yakima. "We've fallen in love with the place," he says. Anna is the school counselor at Tieton Elementary School, and Nate is design director at Yakima Housing Authority (YHA). He describes this position as "a natural progression" after his fellowship. "The initial idea [behind the Rose Fellowship] was that affordable housing needed more rigorous design and that designers, if they're trained well, make good developers," Nate says. "The fellowship exists to meld those two worlds more seamlessly, and where I am today is a perfect case in point: I'm at YHA to infuse more design rigor into all the housing we're building."

One of YHA's recent projects is a community center that will provide space for social gatherings and training on critical workplace issues such as pesticide management and forklift operation. He is also working with the City of Granger to get a Community Development Block Grant to fund the installation of sidewalks that connect stores and existing infrastructure in the town, as well as adopt the Safe Routes to School program, which would provide a traffic light at the intersection where children cross.

"The stories of migrants coming to America today are as much a part of our identity as the history of migration from our ancestors," Nate says. "There are so many stories you don't hear, but it makes me want to push even more into the valley to hear these stories, generational stories like Sandra's and Amanda's. Because for almost all of us, if you trace your history back far enough, in one way or another you are a part of the migrant story."

6
6

Harvest of the hops, Moxee, Wash.

Detroit, Michigan

"It's like a miracle, really," says lifelong Detroiter and community activist Stephanie Harbin. "Just to see the vibrancy come back, and see that people want to come to our city."

The city of Detroit has been suffering from widespread urban blight for decades, and in 2013 it filed for the largest municipal bankruptcy in US history. Many people assumed this signaled the demise of a city that in the 1950s was home to almost two million. And indeed, in recent years America's beloved "Motor City" and the birthplace of Motown saw its population drop below 700,000, leaving many neighborhoods abandoned and businesses shuttered.

But thanks to organizations such as the Detroit Collaborative Design Center (DCDC) and the work of dedicated residents, community activists, city leaders, developers, and investors, Detroit is now known for its robust revitalization.

Stephanie, who has lived on San Juan Drive for fifty years and serves as its block club president, got involved with the DCDC when she and Fitzgerald neighborhood resident Gaston Nash applied for a neighborhood improvement grant through Kresge Innovative Projects: Detroit. They partnered with DCDC to rehabilitate debris-choked and overgrown alleyways and activate vacant lots in the neighborhood.

Over the past few decades, community design centers such as the DCDC have emerged to work alongside community development corporations (CDCs) to provide low- and moderate-income areas with broader access to design services in planning, urban design, and infrastructure. Community design centers also serve as a vital nexus for residents, community stakeholders, design professionals, urban planners, nonprofits, local government, and other institutions to collaborate and create effective solutions delivered directly to the local community.

In a city where neighborhoods span 139 square miles and the majority of investment is downtown, DCDC is playing an outsized role in the city's transformation. Founded in 1994, the nonprofit is a full-service architecture and urban design firm at the University of Detroit's Mercy School of Architecture. It employs seven full-time urban design, architecture, and landscape architecture professionals, and two to four student interns. The emphasis is on collaboration: DCDC works with residents to facilitate their own process of planning, development, and building design.

Ceara O'Leary, whose 2012–2014 Rose Fellowship was hosted by DCDC, is now the organization's co-executive director. She says, "It's essential for community members to be able to shape the decision-making that happens in the built environment in their neighborhoods as a justice issue. . . . I believe that everybody should live in strong,

Opposite: Stephanie Harbin, President, San Juan Block Club

FITZGERALD
welcome to th
FITZGERALD NEIG

Mural: *The Healing Wall*; Artist: The Alley Project (TAP), Grace In Action Church, Southwest Detroit

Demolition, in 2014, of the Brewster-Douglass Housing Projects, built 1935–1955

The Brilliant Detroit House in the Fitzgerald Community

healthy neighborhoods, and neighbors should be part of shaping what that looks like. And that's a process we can help facilitate."

Ceara arrived in Detroit just before the bankruptcy. "There was this big, optimistic planning effort happening then," she says. In the first few months of her Rose Fellowship, Ceara jumped into the Detroit Works Project Long Term Planning team, helping to host twenty planning meetings and getting to know leaders across the city. She started building relationships that remain strong to this day. "The Detroit Works Project allowed me to meet and work with key community leaders really early, which has been instrumental," she says.

Josh Budiongan was a design consultant with DCDC prior to his 2015–2017 Rose Fellowship with Jefferson East, Inc. (JEI), a multiservice neighborhood organization serving Detroit's east side. Now DCDC's designer and project manager, Josh put together a development framework for Jefferson East, which helped attract an unprecedented $50 million in investments and the first restaurant in Jefferson Chalmers in decades, Norma G's.

"I really believe that everybody should live in strong, healthy neighborhoods, and neighbors should be part of shaping what that looks like. And that's a process we can help facilitate." —Ceara O'Leary

Owned by Trinidadian-born Lester Gouvia, the restaurant started as a food truck business, cooking his mom's Trinidadian recipes out of a repurposed teal, bright yellow, and fuchsia DHL truck. Opening a permanent Norma G's was a dream come true. "One of the rules I always got from my family was, if you're going to cook, do it with love," says Lester. "If you don't have the love, don't go in there. It doesn't make sense."

Josh and the JEI team helped Lester convert a neighborhood bank into the restaurant, but going from food truck to brick and mortar wasn't easy. It's one thing to draw a neighborhood plan that promotes local retail and restaurants, and another to take the risk of opening a new business.

"At first it's words, and then how do those words actually manifest into action?" Lester says. "I feel for people, others who are trying this. Because as the city's changing . . . it's going to become even more difficult, more expensive." JEI supported Lester through the complicated process of permits, licenses, funding, and construction. After numerous delays and setbacks, the restaurant opened in August 2018 and is thriving. "I think Detroiters are just tenacious and creative and always looking to grow or do something big," says Josh. "The community hasn't had a business like Norma G's in over thirty years, a place to have a casual fine-dining experience, or a place to meet your neighbors and interact with them that isn't some dumpy dive bar."

Given their passionate commitment to Detroit, it is no surprise that Stephanie, Ceara, and Josh have collaborated on many initiatives and continue to work together. In 2019, the group spearheaded the San Juan Community Block Club's Community Hub, which is being designed and built in partnership with DCDC, community members, the city planning department, the Detroit Mercy School of Architecture, and student designers, whom Josh supervises. The new pavilion provides space for neighborhood barbecues, retirement gatherings, parties, block club meetings, and concerts.

Children at the Ella Fitzgerald Park

Ceara O'Leary, Rose Fellow, 2012–2014

h Budiongan, Rose Fellow,
5–2017

Ribbon cutting of Norma G's restaurant: Joshua Elling, Executive Director, Jefferson East Inc., Detroit Mayor Mike Duggan, Lester Gouvia, owner, Derric Scott, East Jefferson Development Company, Mike Rafferty, New Detroit (left to right)

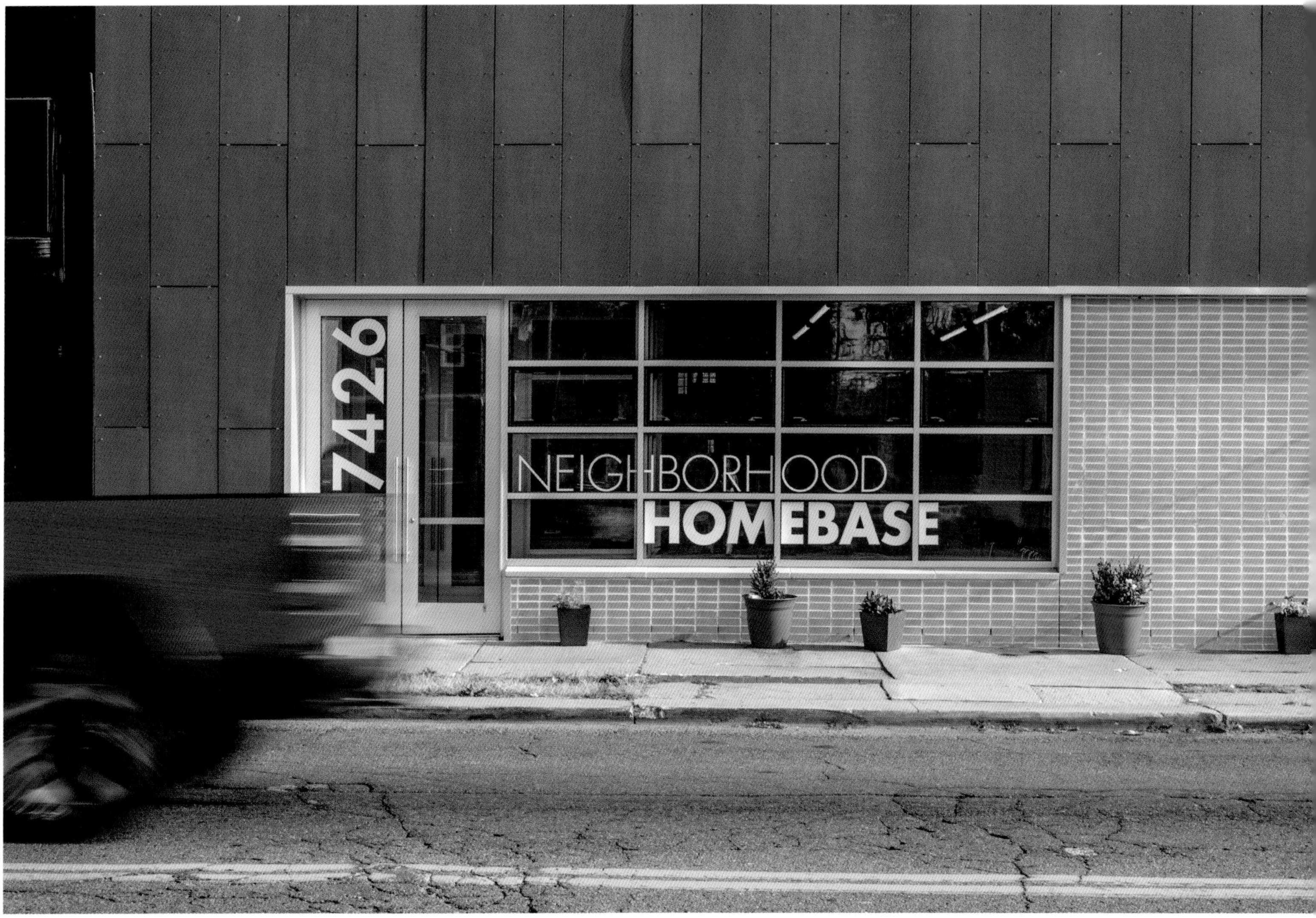
7426
NEIGHBORHOOD
HOMEBASE

"I'm excited about this," says Stephanie. "And one thing I am really pleased with, and want to stress, is that all these projects are community driven." Stephanie is right to point this out: it's the love and commitment of community members who decided to stay that's driving Detroit's revitalization. "There's a lot of things that make Detroit special," says Ceara, "but from my experience, it's the neighbors and the community members who have been leading neighborhood work for so long. It's the people who make this city special—they're the heart of the city for sure."

One of DCDC's most recent accomplishments is the opening of Neighborhood HomeBase, a storefront community space housed in a long-vacant former tuxedo shop in the heart of the Livernois-McNichols area. HomeBase serves as an information hub for residents; the home of Live6 Alliance, a nonprofit community planning and development organization; and a satellite site for DCDC.

"It will be really impactful to be off campus and embedded in the community where we're doing work," Ceara says. "We'll be more accessible to community members and leaders, more visible, and more present." Neighborhood HomeBase provides shared work desks and meeting space so residents, neighborhood groups, members of local government, and nonprofits can easily interact with one another.

"To me, this is the beauty of architecture and is what we should aspire to do with the buildings we design—to have that connection," says Josh. "The notion of designing a space collaboratively and having it tell the story of [the participants] together—HomeBase is that."

Among her many activities, Stephanie serves as "space ambassador" at HomeBase, scheduling events for Detroit block clubs and nonprofit organizations. "It's like a revolving door in there," she says. "Just so much activity, for multiple reasons. Any resource that has come into our community, HomeBase can direct you."

The Detroit Collaborative Development Center exemplifies community-driven design at its best. Through the work of countless residents such as Stephanie and dedicated partners such as Ceara and Josh, the story of Detroit is shifting from a cautionary tale of a once-great city that fell into ruin, to a hopeful narrative of a great American city with a promising future.

Owner and visitors of Eric's I've Been Framed, during the Light Up Livernois event, Livernois Avenue, Detroit's Historic Avenue of Fashion

NIKE

Seattle, Washington

"I actually still get that, wherever I go," Rose Fellow Joann Ware says. "If I tell people I'm from Olympia, they usually say, 'No, really, where are you *really* from?' The inference, of course, is that I'm not 'really' an American."

Growing up in a predominantly white community in Olympia, Washington, Joann was often asked where she was from. Her parents, first-generation Taiwanese immigrants, moved to the United States in the 1970s to pursue higher education.

She describes feeling like an outsider in her own community because of the implied otherness in these questions. She says, "I am American, even though I have brown skin and dark features. People don't ask [my husband] these types of questions—they just assume he's American. People of color all over the country still experience microaggressions like this, as well as overt racism today. It is not something that's just in history."

About 60 miles away in Seattle's International District, commonly known as the ID, Joann "could see people who looked like me." On Saturdays, Joann, her parents, and her brother made the trip to Chinatown, as they called it then, to do their shopping, eat at a favorite restaurant, and go to the bookstore for newspapers from Taiwan. The only source of news before the internet, the papers were passed from person to person throughout the small Chinese and Taiwanese American community back in Olympia.

These Saturday trips were a highlight of Joann's childhood. She loved to peruse Chinese-language picture books, music tapes, and craft books at the store where her parents got their newspapers and videos. At the Chinese school in the ID, Joann participated in language and calligraphy competitions. She witnessed her mother become a US citizen in the immigration building on 4th Street. For Joann and her family, the ID felt like home.

"My parents wanted me to be exposed to the culture as a kid, which is why they made the long drive each week," says Joann. "In the end, it stuck and the ID became a meaningful place for me."

When Joann attended the University of Washington, the ID took on a different meaning for her. It was where she hung out with friends to drink bubble tea and get late-night food after going out. After graduating from UW and starting a new job in Tacoma, she drove all the way back to the ID to celebrate her first paycheck by taking her friends out to a Chinese banquet dinner.

Joann then traveled east to the Rhode Island School of Design (RISD) for her master's degree in architecture, where her thesis was about how immigrants and refugees

Joann Ware, Rose Fellow, 2010–2013

navigated life in Providence. When a professor told her about the Rose Fellowship at the Interim Community Development Association in the ID, Joann says, "it felt like fate."

At the time, Joann was not aware of "public interest" design practices and had no idea that designing affordable housing could be a viable career path. But she leapt at the chance to work in the neighborhood where she had grown up in so many ways.

Seattle's International District has a complex history. Today it is experiencing intense pressure from developers wanting to build more hotels and high-rise, market-rate apartments for workers in Seattle's technology economy. But for the past century, it was one of the only places in the region where people of Asian-Pacific Islander descent were allowed to live.

Chinese immigrants first came to the Pacific Northwest in the 1860s, creating an initial Chinatown by the waterfront. Anti-Chinese sentiment rose as the US experienced an economic downturn in the 1870s and 1880s, resulting in the Chinese Exclusion Act of 1882. For ten years it suspended the immigration of Chinese laborers, who were seen as a threat to American jobs. In 1886, a violent mob removed many of Seattle's remaining Chinese residents. Federal troops were dispatched to restore order. It took two decades for the Chinese population to return to 1885 levels,[1] and these residents constructed a second Chinatown farther inland. The third, and current, location is along King Street in the ID.

Several other Asian immigrant populations have also established communities in the ID. The first Japanese immigrants in Seattle were mostly single men working in canneries, railroading, and the massive logging industry, jobs left open by the Chinese Exclusion Act of 1882. These early residents established Nihonmachi, or Japantown, which thrived for decades until the World War II internment of Japanese Americans forced the 8,000 members of Seattle's Japanese community to abandon their homes and businesses and move to internment camps in Idaho and elsewhere. Later, Vietnamese immigrants arriving in the mid-1970s established Little Saigon. Today, Chinatown, Nihonmachi, and Little Saigon are the three largest areas in the ID, but many others of Asian-Pacific Islander descent live and work in this multi-ethnic area.

For her Rose Fellowship, Joann partnered with Interim CDA. This nonprofit advocates for low- and moderate-income Asian and Pacific Islander communities in the Puget Sound area. Interim's roots go back to 1969, when community activists and business leaders organized to revitalize Seattle's Chinatown. Because of economic decline and the construction of Interstate 5, which bisected the neighborhood, scores of apartments, hotels, and businesses closed, causing the wide-scale displacement of residents.

Since then, Interim CDA has been a mainstay, adapting to meet evolving community needs such as financial literacy, homelessness, environmental justice, and a lack of affordable housing. The organization has renovated or constructed 303 affordable-housing units and has been involved in the renovation of an additional 195 units.[2] They own five affordable-housing buildings, four of them in the ID, which provide permanent housing for more than 900 people each year.[3]

One of Joann's major projects was the development of Hirabayashi Place, a multi-family building at the corner of 4th and South Main Streets that fills a gap between

Canton Alley, International District

extremely low-income housing and market-rate housing. The original design, created by the Seattle firm Mithun in 2010, called for a mix of studios and one- and two-bedroom units, for a total of ninety-six units offered at 40–60 percent of the area median income (AMI).

"Our ultimate goals included preserving a sense of community, healthy residents, and a durable building that visibly demonstrated innovative sustainable strategies," Joann says. "And my personal goal was to see this project through construction."

At first, things went according to plan. "We obtained site control of the final parcel [in 2011], three days before the application due date," Joann says. "Our team showed up at King County Trustees sale with $800,000 in cashiers' checks from Impact Capital and a whole bunch of lawyers to bid on the parcel. Luckily, we were unopposed, so then we were the proud owners of a rundown nightclub building."

Much of 2011 was dedicated to fundraising and working with Mithun and Walsh Construction to establish a design and cost estimate that reflected InterIm CDA's construction standards. The plan also needed to meet "green checklists," such as the Evergreen Sustainable Development Standards.[4]

The end of 2011 brought bad news. First, a key team member at InterIm CDA left abruptly. A week later, the Washington State Housing Finance Commission published the list of projects receiving Housing Trust funding, and the 4th and Main development was not among them. "This news was extremely crushing for me," says Joann, "because the next trust fund biennial funding round in 2013 put project construction completion well beyond my fellowship term."

The next year, however, brought positive developments. In 2012, the building was named Hirabayashi Place in honor of a local hero, Gordon Kiyoshi Hirabayashi. A Seattle native, Hirabayashi received his PhD in sociology from the University of Washington. He is best known for boldly defying the mass internment of Japanese Americans during World War II and for the 1943 court case that bears his name, *Hirabayashi v. United States*. The Supreme Court ruled against him and he was incarcerated, but his wrongful conviction was overturned in 1987. Hirabayashi died in 2012 at age ninety-three, and in 2018 he was posthumously awarded the Presidential Medal of Freedom for his "open defiance of discrimination against Japanese Americans" and his pursuit of justice.

A crucial next step was applying for a 4-percent Low Income Housing Tax Credit (LIHTC)[5] with the Washington State Housing Finance Commission. The LIHTC program is something nearly every Rose Fellow learns to negotiate.

As part of the Tax Reform Act of 1986, low-income housing tax credits are allocated by state housing-finance agencies to developers of rental housing, who are awarded the credits through a competitive application process and judged according to the priorities of each state's Qualified Allocation Plan (QAP). The QAP is a powerful tool for promoting best practices in affordable-housing design, since QAP guidelines may include incentives and requirements around sustainability measures or providing amenities for the populations being served.

Nonprofit developers can partner with investors to exchange the value of the future tax credits for the equity money needed to design and build income-restricted rental housing. Tax credit syndicators, such as Enterprise Community Partners, facilitate

Inside the Uwajimaya Market, International District

this transaction by connecting developers with tax credits to investors and ensuring the partnership is consistent with Department of Treasury regulations.

Properties developed or rehabilitated using low-income-housing tax credits can be rented only to families with earnings at or below 60 percent of AMI.[6] According to the latest statistics, the LIHTC program was responsible for the creation of an average of more than 1,411 projects and 107,000 units per year between 1995 and 2017.[7]

There are two kinds of LIHTC—9 percent and 4 percent. Equity covers about 70 percent of the development cost for a project funded with 9 percent LIHTC, and about 30 percent of projects funded with 4 percent LIHTC, such as Hirabayashi Place.

James Madden, senior program director for Enterprise's Seattle office, points out that in Washington, where the housing crisis is extreme, the QAP and policies for 9 percent credits target projects that serve very low-income households (0–50 percent of AMI) or formerly homeless people. The 4 percent credits are more often used for workforce housing—housing for low-to-moderate-income families and individuals who want to live near their place of employment. The LIHTC program in Washington is "always oversubscribed," Madden says.

To prepare for their 4 percent LIHTC application, Joann and her team submitted a Total Cost Limit Waiver request, which included a detailed cost analysis supporting their cost per unit. It also included a justification for why a project using Version 2.0 of the Evergreen Sustainable Development Standard, with many more mandatory green building requirements, would cost more to develop than a project using Version 1.2.

"Our ultimate goals included preserving a sense of community, healthy residents, and a durable building that visibly demonstrated innovative sustainable strategies. And my personal goal was to see this project through construction."
—Joann Ware

The next challenge was an unexpected request from public funders to include a no-parking option, which required a complete redesign of the building's first two stories. The requirement to provide on-site parking is one of the most contentious issues in affordable-housing development. Cities and states have different requirements, from one-half to two parking spaces per unit. Additional cars and increased traffic are common neighborhood objections to new affordable-housing developments. Structured parking spaces can cost $30,000–$60,000 per space, adding a significant strain on the total development cost. Enterprise Green Communities Criteria[8] requires that affordable-housing developments be located in amenity-rich neighborhoods with access to transit options. This ensures that residents can thrive even if they don't own a car.

On the positive side, the redesign added eleven units and the potential to incorporate Housing First units, which would offer unhoused people a place to live as quickly as possible, as well as supportive services. The additional units also contributed to the project's eligibility for tax credits and increased the Total Cost Limit Waiver threshold.

By the end of 2012, funding came through in $2.5 million from the Washington State Housing Trust Fund, $5.6 million from the Seattle Office of Housing, and $650,000 from King County.

In the final year of Joann's Rose Fellowship, however, Seattle was in the midst of a building boom for recession-stalled projects, leaving Joann and the design team grappling with skyrocketing construction bids. To cut costs, the design team and the general contractor pared the project down to a bare-bones building.

With a new round of funding applications submitted in September 2013, Joann turned her attention to other tasks associated with Hirabayashi Place, such as historical-design review, commercial-space programming, ongoing community engagement, and public artwork. The development team assembled a community group to guide the incorporation of social justice into the building through art and design.

"I was most excited about the work with the Hirabayashi Place Legacy of Justice, which was a group of community members who volunteered to steward a series of educational events and exhibitions in the building to celebrate the work of Gordon Hirabayashi and social justice," Joann says. "Public art on or around the building was a major component of this project."

The Legacy of Justice group began with *Stand Up for Social Justice*, a temporary origami installation composed of 3,000 community-made paper cranes, led by Interim CDA real-estate development director Leslie Morishita. It engaged many local artists and residents in projects that explored the history and cultural identity of Nihonmachi and imparted a sense of their meaning in this historic neighborhood.

As construction on Hirabayashi Place continued, Joann began working with Interim CDA's Wilderness Inner-City Leadership Development (WILD) program to create a series of murals celebrating Gordon Hirabayashi, to hang on the vacant buildings and construction fencing. The youth were able to link Gordon's stand against injustice to the opportunities they have as first- and second-generation Asian Americans.

Though Joann's Rose Fellowship came to a close at the end of 2013, she remained with Interim CDA to see the construction of Hirabayashi Place through to completion. The setbacks and delays, though frustrating, allowed Joann and the design team to devote time to enhance the design of the Legacy of Justice project, and throughout it all, they remained committed to their environmental and programmatic goals.

Hirabayashi Place was finally completed in early 2016, adding a mixed-use, transit-oriented, workforce housing development with ninety-six apartments to the ID. It also features a trilingual preschool where Mandarin, Spanish, and English are spoken. The school is on the ground floor and the playground is on the roof, where the incredible view of Seattle is reserved for the children and teachers.

The facade design, by Casey Huang of Mithun, includes window modulation based on Shoji screens, and an indigo-and-white pattern based on traditional textiles. The League of Justice placed five permanent public art installations at the building, and it hosts ongoing educational forums that teach visitors and residents about Gordon Hirabayashi's legacy, as well as the culture and history of Nihonmachi, Seattle's Japantown.

"Hirabayashi's story resonates with me because he's what we all hope to be in the work that we do," Joann says. "Even though folks aren't being mass incarcerated at the scale people were during the World War II internment period, there are injustices that are still happening to people of color in the ID that organizations like Interim CDA are

nstallation: *Portrait of Gordon Hirabayashi*; Artists: Yoko Fedorenko and Hana Fedorenko

Above and opposite: Hirabayashi Place, Seattle. Developer: InterIm CDA; Architect: Mithun

HIRABAYASHI PLACE 平林プレース

Joann Ware with her son, Eddie

really working to fight." One of those injustices, tragically, is not in the least new: the ongoing threat of resident displacement. "Asian-Pacific Islanders are getting pushed out to different parts of the region as they're getting priced out of the ID—or actually getting priced out of Seattle altogether," Joann says.

If past neighborhood displacement came from discriminatory laws, the current threats come from rezoning, rising costs, profit-driven development, and the demand for market-rate and luxury housing. Joann acknowledges that the neighborhood is constantly changing and "should not be a museum," but she and many others are watching prices escalate and rents become unaffordable for both residents and small businesses.

Valued for its diverse, unique, and robust culture, the International District is in jeopardy of losing the very conditions that formed it. Even now, a new high-rise, market-rate condominium building is going up next door to Hirabayashi Place, casting shadows on the rooftop preschool playground.

Yet to Joann, the community still feels like home. "It feels to me like a true neighborhood," she says, "like a super-walkable neighborhood that other neighborhoods should be modeling themselves after, because there's grocery stores and clinics and all the things you need within a four-block radius of each other."

Joann and her husband regularly bring their son to experience the ID, as her parents did for her. "I want my son to know that Lunar New Year firecrackers and dragon dances are just as American as trick-or-treating at Halloween," Joann says. "I want him to be proud of being Asian American and not to let anyone doubt his Americanness. The ID offers a place where the culture is thriving, and it allows the broader community a chance to experience Asian American culture and understand it is an integral part of American culture."

What's abundantly clear is that even throughout its complex history, the ID is intact as a home for multiple ethnicities, low-income families, elders, immigrants, and refugees. This has been accomplished through collaboration across many ethnic groups and the dedicated work of countless residents and community activists.

"I wanted to be a Rose Fellow because I felt like architecture could do so much more for society than what I was seeing," Joann says. "I got a glimpse of that at Interim CDA. Now, I'm continuing to do that work, but as an architect on affordable housing." Her work with the architecture firm Schemata Workshop is a natural extension of her work as a Rose Fellow.

"It was through the Rose Fellowship that I learned that a great design can only help those in need if it is built," says Joann. "It is just a beautiful drawing otherwise."

Mississippi Delta

"We always want to design and build housing and address housing and economic structural inequities, but we think those two things are really inseparable," says Rose Fellow Emily Roush-Elliott of Delta Design Build.

In the Mississippi Delta, housing may be affordable, but the conditions can be so substandard there are few good places to live. The area suffers from a long history of systematized inequity, ranging from legislation that excluded domestic and farm labor from social security, to more-insidious conditions such as a continued attachment to a state flag that is largely composed of the Confederate symbol. This inequity continually undermines opportunities to build economic stability and pass along generational wealth.

Baptist Town is one of the oldest African American neighborhoods in Greenwood, Mississippi. It is known as a close-knit community and as the stomping grounds of blues legends such as Robert Johnson, Honeyboy Edwards, and Sonnyboy Williamson.

Baptist Town is also a place so "frozen in time"[1] that many scenes from *The Help*, set in 1960s Jackson, Mississippi, were filmed here in 2010. Still highly segregated and cut off from the city's downtown by railroad tracks and a bayou, the neighborhood suffers from inadequate infrastructure, high unemployment, a lack of opportunity, and the blight of dilapidated and abandoned homes.

In 2000, the Greenwood-Leflore-Carroll Economic Development Foundation, in partnership with the Carl Small Town Center, the Foundation for the Mid-South, the Fuller Center for Housing, and Enterprise Community Partners, launched the Baptist Town Neighborhood Reinvestment project. Its objective was addressing the long-standing issues that plagued residents—chief among them a lack of affordable homes built to withstand the region's extreme weather events.

Over the next decade, many university groups and architecture students traveled to Baptist Town to study the neighborhood and determine how best to help. Various development plans were drawn up and community engagement initiatives launched, but the students left when the semester ended, and little lasting progress was made.

In 2013, when Emily and her husband, Richard Elliott, left her hometown of Cincinnati and moved to Greenwood for her three-year Rose Fellowship, they found a place still so underresourced that Emily describes it as being in "a fight for normalcy." Emily had been in Greenwood only two days when her new boss, Angela Curry, executive director of the Greenwood-Leflore-Carroll EDF, asked her, "Emily, are you going to stay?" Angela and many other residents of Greenwood and the larger

Opposite: Lillie Mae Calbert, at her home in Eastmoor Estates, Moorhead, MS

Beverly Reans, postal carrier, on Stephens Avenue in Baptist Town, Greenwood, MS

Mississippi Delta had become accustomed to departures: organizations and individuals came and went, and residents who had the opportunity to leave did so.

Emily and Richard, however, had a different philosophy, deeply informed by their work with a Cincinnati-based organization called Village Life Outreach Project, which partners with communities in the Rorya District of Tanzania on sustainable projects to fight poverty and improve health, water quality and quantity, and educational outcomes. Emily's work with Village Life began in 2010 and continues to this day, and one of the principles she learned there was to have no exit strategy.

Often in the field of community development, we speak about the desire to become obsolete, to no longer be needed. The Village Life approach is radically different. Yes, make conditions better. Yes, learn from those efforts. But there will always be new and shifting needs in a community, and committing to stay acknowledges this as a reality. Another principle Emily learned from Village Life was to bring a deep and familial humility to her work. Emily and her team aren't offering solutions; they are offering help. The work is never done, and they tell community members they can always call.

As a Rose Fellow, Emily inherited a stalled-out effort to utilize Katrina Cottages—the healthier, more permanent second iteration of the FEMA trailer—as permanent affordable housing. In keeping with the disposition plan for the Mississippi Alternative Housing Program (MAHP),[2] twenty-six of the modular homes had been donated to the Greenwood in 2011.

Without a housing developer on the project team, the web of necessary approvals and processes had stalled, and time was running out on a nearly half-million-dollar grant to cover the cost of foundations and related installation work for the cottages.

Emily persevered, supported by the network of the Rose Fellowship; Hope Enterprise Corporation; Bruce Tolar, an architect with experience permanently setting the modular homes; the Neighborhood Development Foundation; and others. Alongside local partners, she overcame long delays in state legislature approvals by lobbying lawmakers and other officials.

She organized funding and made sure there were affordable mortgages for residents. She managed and did installation work with Richard, a licensed contractor, and hired as many people from Baptist Town as she could, knowing that training and jobs are an important path to escaping poverty. She got this team to renovate the community center, refurbish a playground and parts of the local park, and design and construct other beautification projects.

Emily was asked continually if she was going to leave. But she and Richard remained, knowing that the best way to gain trust was to show that they were going to be a consistent presence. They shifted their roles as needed—providing help with design, planning, policy, economic development, and community organizing. Perhaps most important, they learned that in the Mississippi Delta, community development has to be *economic* development first, and that it should never be separated from affordable housing.

George Holland, mayor of nearby Moorhead, was one of a dozen children and the son of a sharecropper. He started picking cotton at age eight. He laughs now, recounting that he was "an exceptionally good cotton picker" and bought his first bike for $10 after

A finished Katrina Cottage, Baptist Town

Emily Roush-Elliott, Rose Fellow, 2013–2015

a season of picking. He also remembers being poor, "but we didn't know we were poor because our family sheltered us," he says.

This is a refrain Emily has heard many times. "I haven't met anyone in this community who describes themselves as poor or low income," Emily says. George's family is a success story. In 1964, with money he'd saved from sharecropping, his father was able to purchase a home. He died shortly thereafter, but the home he secured stabilized the family and set them on a path of success. George eventually married, and he and his wife built careers in Chicago and St. Louis. Then in 2005, he had "a vision about coming back to Mississippi" to help his home community. Convincing his wife to move was another matter, but he says, "the idea of building a new home" appealed to her and she "decided we could try it."

His story is the exception, and it's fascinating to consider how much of his success was connected to having a stable home. Emily agrees. "I think [moving away] is the measure of success for a lot of people," she says, "primarily African American people who grew up in this town, this region." She is careful to clarify that she doesn't discourage people from leaving. "But what if we can change the narrative just a little bit and say, 'I can see a version of success that means I don't have to leave'?" she says. "That's what excites me and keeps me here."

Indeed, many people leave the Delta because decent housing is scarce. Gregory Flippins, director of the Greenwood Housing Authority, shared that of the 260 vouchers his organization manages, 5 percent (thirteen families) live outside Greenwood because they can't find a home that meets the minimum standards required by the US Department of Housing and Urban Development (HUD) Section 8 Housing Choice Voucher program.[3] When Emily and Richard arrived in 2013, the population of Greenwood was between 16,000 and 17,000 people. Today it's less than 14,000.[4]

There have been efforts to fill this housing gap. In 1969, two white brothers developed Eastmoor Estates, a subdivision of eighty-four ranch houses outside Moorhead, a small town about 25 miles west of Greenwood, with loans from the Federal Housing Administration (FHA) and rent subsidies from HUD. But the site was suspect from the beginning. First, its location just outside city limits seemed intentional, given that the Voting Rights Act of 1965 had recently been passed. The new residents would not be able to vote in the city. Second, an unusual agreement was struck between the local governing bodies. The city would be responsible for sewer and water, and the county would tend to the storm sewer and roads. Instead of both parties sharing responsibility, eventually, neither provided these services. What's more, Eastmoor Estates was built below the floodplain, leading to long-term construction and flooding issues.

Emma Bush was one of the early renters, and Eastmoor was a revelation to her. "Where I come from, we didn't have bathrooms," she says. "We didn't have running water. When they built these low-income houses, that was the best thing that could have happened." At that time, Emma was recently married, and she and her husband moved shortly before their first child was born. Forty-seven years later, she has raised her children, grandchildren, and now great-grandchildren in that same house.

Over those years, however, the homes fell into grave disrepair, victim to the owners' neglect and political geography. By 2006, there were deep potholes in the streets and

George Holland, mayor, in front of the mural that he painted in downtown Moorhead

Lagwunda (Shea) Clark at her home in Eastmoor Estates

no overhead streetlights, which made going outside dangerous. "The roads were so bad you were scared to walk across them at night," Emma says. "There were potholes so big you would fall in and break your leg." Worse, the substandard construction and faulty infrastructure resulted in heaving and destabilized walls, and raw sewage bubbling up in the yards, streets, and sidewalks. No one could walk outside because of the unbearable stench. Emma's husband found himself constantly fighting the sewage. One day in 2006, he was digging in their front yard to try once again to repair a sewer pipe. Shortly after going inside to rest, he passed away of a massive heart attack.

Meanwhile, a new owner, Glen Miller, acquired Eastmoor Estates in 1993 with funding from the Low-Income Housing Tax Credit Program (LIHTC), promising to rehabilitate it. Miller made little to no investment but received another infusion of cash from tax credits between 1994 and 2000. Were it not for the raw sewage in bathtubs and flowing in the streets, it is possible that no one would have noticed.

But Congressman Bennie Thompson visited in 2001 and declared the property unlivable. Federal funding was withdrawn, and Miller promptly sent a letter to tenants that there were no more federal funds available for Section 8 vouchers and that homeowners either had to move out or buy their homes. Many chose to stay and buy—it was their home and their neighborhood—but this was also a scam. According to resident Lagwunda (Shea) Clark, they were paying $300 to $500 per month in "mortgage" to Miller, but they never had their names on the deed.

"We work at the intersection of market forces and public interest. Our work is led by our values that waste is a social construct, process is as important as product, and design responses must be unique and grounded in local conditions."
—Emily Roush-Elliott

This was the level of desperation when help finally arrived. Desiree Hensley was an associate professor at the University of Mississippi School of Law and director of the Housing Clinic. After hearing about the conditions, she made a visit, and that was enough: she committed to representing this community pro bono.

With Desiree providing guidance, Shea, president of the Eastmoor Residents' Association, hosted the first community meeting. Only a half-dozen people showed up, including Emma Bush and Johnny Carter. People were skeptical. Emma remembers the general attitude being "What makes you think you can go against that rich white man?"

After a year of legal analysis, Desiree and the Housing Clinic filed a lawsuit on behalf of the neighborhood against the city of Moorhead, Sunflower County, and the private landowner. The lawsuit cost the residents' association $300, which came out to about $8 per household, but given the skepticism and cost, many households were unable or chose not to contribute their $8 share. The residents' association combined resources on behalf of the community to start the process.

With Shea's house serving as headquarters, the residents endured pushback and threats of eviction. Shea says, "At one point, it did get kind of scary because we were at the point where Glen Miller had a lady working for him who would bring eviction notices probably three times a week." And all the while, the neighborhood continued to crumble.

Above and opposite: Renovation of homes by Delta Design Build Workshop

Michelle Stadelman, Rose Fellow, 2017–2019 (top right), with Delta Design Build Workshop team Richard Elliott, Jeremiah Whitehead, William Adams, Emily Roush-Elliott, and Dontavius McLemore (clockwise from top left)

After four long years of litigation, however, the case was settled in favor of the residents. The city would fix the sewer system, the county would fix the roads, and residents who had participated in the lawsuit would get the deed to their houses.

Though these were big wins in the fight for basic housing and infrastructure that most Americans take for granted, many of the homes were physically shifting in the expansive soil of the former floodplain. The buildings needed comprehensive structural rehabilitation. Fortunately, with the new homes in Baptist Town occupied, and owners paying on their mortgages, Emily, Richard, and their team could turn their attention to Eastmoor.

Overwhelmed by the funding needed to complete the repair work, they reached out to friends at Hope Enterprise Corporation, which was in the process of identifying new housing projects to lead in the Delta. Within months, Phil Eide, Hope's senior vice president of community and economic development, and founder and CEO William (Bill) Bynum secured a grant from Goldman Sachs. Those funds supported the rehabilitation of forty homes; additional public and philanthropic resources funded the resurfacing of sidewalks and roads and a new playground that local children helped design.[5]

"Eastmoor is a great example of where a residents' association banded together and created change," Emily says. "People have such pride in those houses because they're theirs."

Not only are Emily and Richard not leaving, they are digging in deep. They joined a church where Emily gives the Sunday children's sermon a few times a year. To continue their work after her fellowship ended, the couple founded their own company, the Delta Design Build Workshop (Delta DB). At first, they took on a few traditional design and construction projects to continue to employ their team of neighborhood residents and understand the limits of what their business could offer. But over time, it became clear that with the partnerships and knowledge they had gained during Emily's fellowship, Delta DB could focus on the type of work they value most.

"We work at the intersection of market forces and public interest," Emily says. "Our work is led by our values that waste is a social construct, process is as important as product, and design responses must be unique and grounded in local conditions." The team has been able to work entirely on community-focused projects since late 2016.

These values are often applied person by person, conversation by conversation, one issue at a time. I had the chance to sit on the front porch with Emily and a Baptist Town homeowner who had recently retired as a domestic aide for a wealthy white family in town. She bought her home in 2014 and has a mortgage and insurance, which she pays conscientiously a few days before it is due. She and Emily spoke about her need for a will, to ensure that at her death the house conveys to her son. I see the granular nature of the work happening in Greenwood: a front porch, a conversation, one-on-one life planning, one step at a time.

Similarly, step by step, one person at a time, Emily and Richard have built a team. Many of the young men who work or have worked at Delta DB have lost a parent to violence. Benjamin Jaboree Kinds (BJ) is one of them. Born in 1997 in Jackson, Mississippi, BJ has faced significant adversity. His father is serving a life sentence for

Richard Elliott, Delta Design Build Workshop

Benjamin Jaboree "BJ" Kinds, Delta Design Build Workshop

killing his mother. BJ and his sister now live in an apartment. The rent is relatively high, and while property maintenance is better than it once was in Eastmoor, it is still deplorable. Over the three years BJ has been working with Delta DB, however, he has earned his GED and driver's license and opened checking and savings accounts. On my most recent visit, he and Emily drove by a house he is considering buying, a small brick ranch near downtown Greenwood. At age twenty-one, BJ has developed alongside Delta DB as he has found a trade, a purpose, and an opportunity to own a home.

Delta DB, now licensed to do both architecture and construction, has a staff of eight and serves the greater Mississippi Delta. While home repair and replacement work in Eastmoor remains the firm's largest current project, other efforts, including the Blight Elimination Program (BEP) and a housing research report, are evidence of future ambitions to increase the amount of safe, healthy, affordable housing in the region.

In 2018, Michelle Stadelman joined the team as a Rose Fellow shared between Delta DB and Hope Enterprise Corporation. Michelle's added capacity has resulted in new or improved community facilities in nine small towns. Her willingness to apply her creative problem-solving skills (refined by over a decade of professional practice and teaching) to everything from pro forma financial analysis to park bench installations is essential to the team's recent successes. Undergirding this technical expertise is Michelle's commitment to individual relationships and respect for clients. Michelle's fellowship ended December 2019, but she has accepted a job offer and plans to stay.

When she first moved to Greenwood seven years ago, Emily was a bit put off by constantly being asked if she was leaving. Now she is comforted by the fact that people see that she and Richard are invested enough to choose Greenwood as their home.

Michelle Whetten, vice president and Gulf Coast market leader for Enterprise Community Partners, says Emily's instincts to be a consistent, long-term presence "were right on. Emily and Richard knew seeing results on the ground—new houses filled with homeowners—would take a long time. They knew it would be important to have small but visible wins." As those wins accumulated—a pocket park, pathways, signage—"residents saw that Emily and Richard were not coming to talk and plan," says Whetten, "they were coming to do and build."

Inspired by this tight-knit community, Emily points out that while "visitors are quick to describe the Mississippi Delta as 'impoverished,' from a nonfinancial-value standpoint the more important values, such as people taking care of each other, community identity, and history and culture, it's incredibly rich." In the Delta, she says, "your well-being and mine are intertwined."

Emma Bush (center), resident, Eastmoor Estates, with grandson, Kelso Bush (left) and son-in-law Patrick Moore (right)

Johnny Carter, resident,
Eastmoor Estates

Kewa Pueblo, New Mexico

"When I introduce myself, I say, 'I'm Joseph Kunkel; I'm a citizen of the Northern Cheyenne Nation.' But by living in these two spaces, I'm acknowledging that I'm of these two worlds and also a citizen of the United States."

Rose Fellow Joseph Kunkel has spent his life and career working out what it means to be a citizen of two nations, and what his obligation is to go back and forth between them. The son of a German Italian father and a mother who was a citizen of the Northern Cheyenne Nation, Joseph spent his formative years in the shore town of Point Pleasant, New Jersey, and the Northern Cheyenne reservation in southeastern Montana.

"That was something that was just very normal, living in these two spaces," he says. At first he wasn't aware of the disparities between his two homes. But as he reached adolescence, the differences between "native and nonnative space" started to become more apparent. Things a teenager took for granted in New Jersey—having a television and reliable internet, for example—were not part of life on the reservation. "Point Pleasant is a very white community that's coming from a place of privilege you don't see on the reservation," he says. While he considers both places home, over the years the reservation has become more home than New Jersey.

In college, Joseph studied architectural engineering and then earned a master's degree in architecture with an emphasis in urban design. "I went from something that was very specific," he says, "to the meta issues we see in urban design and planning—and then I started to combine all of that with Indian country." Having always lived in liminal space, the in-between, he was starting to synthesize the many threads of his experience.

During his second year of architecture school, a summer travel scholarship crystallized the idea for a career in community design. Most recipients used the money to visit Europe, but Joseph had another aim. "I knew the Northern Cheyenne reservation," he says, "but I didn't know Indian country, so this was an opportunity for me to begin to understand what the needs are, and how those needs should be addressed in a native context."

What he found was remarkable similarity among the issues affecting tribal communities. "Housing was an issue," he says. "Political structures were an issue. Government-to-government relationships were an issue. Persistent poverty, food scarcity, health problems—all of these were issues happening all over Indian country. And each community was trying to deal with them in their own way. I also saw that the tools they needed weren't necessarily there."

NEW MEXICO
RAIL RUNNER
1107
NMRX
F
A

AUTHENTIC
INDIAN TRADERS
SANTO DOMINGO INDIAN TRADING POST.

He organized a seminar called Community, Culture, and Place, which brought twelve graduate students to the Northern Cheyenne reservation to explore the ways artists, designers, architects, and communities represent their ideas and aspire to positive social change.

"The seminar was based off a traditional western Beaux-Arts education," he says, "which was my own education at the time, very versed in design theory and practicality. [On the reservation], though, I learned to articulate that in a Native context."

Joseph's graduation in 2009 put him squarely in the midst of a recession, so he spent the next year, once again, between places. This time, it was traveling back and forth between the US and South America, where he worked with and learned from indigenous populations. In the states, he worked part-time for the architecture firm Fielding Nair International in Maryland, helping design and plan three First Nations schools for indigenous Canadian communities.

A second part-time position at the architectural firm Ayers Saint Gross in Washington, DC, left him balancing his time between two entities and "just trying to hustle" as a young designer. When Ayers Saint Gross offered him full-time employment, Joseph moved to DC. It was there, at the 2010 Structures for Inclusion conference hosted by Howard University, that Joseph was introduced to the Enterprise Rose Fellowship and Jamie Blosser, who was among the inaugural class of Rose Fellows from 2000 to 2003. It was the beginning of a fruitful Rose Fellow collaboration that continues to this day. Jamie's host had been the Ohkay Owingeh Housing Authority in Ohkay Owingeh, New Mexico, where she helped develop Tsigo Bugeh (SEE-go BOO-gay) Village, an award-winning, forty-unit affordable-housing development.

In 2009, with initial funding from the National Endowment for the Arts and fiscal sponsorship from Enterprise Community Partners, Jamie launched the Santa Fe–based Sustainable Native Communities Collaborative (SNCC), enlisting Nathaniel Corum, another Rose Fellow alumnus who worked with the Red Feather Development Group based in Bozeman, Montana. At the time, Jamie was an associate at Philadelphia-based Atkin Olshin Schade Architects and director of its Santa Fe office, but she imagined SNCC as a way to move beyond traditional practice to advance the development of culturally and environmentally responsive housing design in American Indian communities. Since then, SNCC has become a leader in disseminating best practices of Native design through research, case studies, tools, and resources for tribal developers.

The conference was a pivotal event for Joseph. Aware that one could spend a lifetime working in any one of the tribal communities, he had already been wondering how to foment "systemic change that [would] bring thought leadership and really move the bar."

The Rose Fellowship was his chance to become deeply embedded in a Native community for an extended period of time. "Before I even got back on the plane after my interview, they called and said my life was going to change," he says. "Soon I was packing up my house in DC and driving through a snowstorm to Santa Fe."

Located about 60 miles from Ohkay Owingeh, between Santa Fe and Albuquerque, Santo Domingo Pueblo was called Gipuy until Spanish conquistadors renamed it Santo Domingo in the seventeenth century. Community members, however, have

eph Kunkel, Rose Fellow,
3–2015

Cynthia Aguilar, librarian,
Kewa Pueblo

always referred to it by its historical Keresan-language name, Kewa Pueblo. After a unanimous 2009 decision from the tribal council, the pueblo officially became known as Kewa Pueblo, though many people, especially nonnatives, still call it Santo Domingo.

The Kewa tribe is known as one of the most conservative Native communities in America, largely closed to outside influence. As a result, they've been able to preserve many elements of their traditional culture, such as the Keresan language. According to some estimates, up to 80 percent of Santo Domingo's children speak Keresan.[1] The tribe is known throughout the world for its magnificent pottery, turquoise jewelry, silver crafts, heishi (bead jewelry), and sacred communal dances. During the annual Green Corn Dance, as many as 2,000 men, women, and children in handmade ceremonial dress dance in unison until dusk, drawing spectators from all over the globe.

Community librarian and eight-year Santo Domingo Housing Authority board member, Cynthia Aguilar, has danced since she was in grade school. "I enjoy it so much," she says. "It's meditative and prayerful. The prayer is really what I am enthused about—I have mindful prayers going throughout the day. Each dance, the songs are different, and when one is in tune with the meaning of the song and you understand every word, you forget about the worries of the world; you are focused on the story. The people who are watching you are giving you that gift. When I hear from spectators that [the dance] was so inspiring, then I know what we have done. I know that we have connected."

Harry and I attended the Corn Dance in August 2019. Tribal members refer to it as a Feast Day, and for good reason. The entire village prepares to host the thousands of visitors who make their way to Santo Domingo to watch the dancing and enjoy a communal feast. Every resident participates: some dance, some perform music, some cook, some serve food.

Feast preparations go on for days, and households collectively host as many as 500 people—many of them strangers—before the day is done. We entered the home of artist and potter Robert Tenorio and discovered that "feast" is an accurate word. Out of what appeared to be a small kitchen came dish after dish—multiple types of chili, enchiladas, posole, many different salads, traditional bread baked in *hornos*, sopapillas, cherries, and desserts. The guests at the table rotated, and new hot dishes kept appearing as we were urged to "Eat, eat."

The next Tuesday, we ate lunch at the home of Manuelita Lovato, an artist and alumnus of the Institute of American Indian Arts. She left the reservation in seventh grade to be schooled at St. Catherine's in Santa Fe and, after retiring from a decades-long career as an arts instructor, returned to the reservation.

During the years she was away, she remained connected to Santo Domingo and its traditions through oral histories passed down through generations, and by coming back to participate in Feast Day. "No matter how many years you're away, home is home and you have to return to the reservation," she says. Over lunch she described how Kewa parents would sit the children down on the floor by the fireplace and tell the stories of their ancestors. "We sat right in front of the fireplace because that's where all the light is coming from," she says, "and we sit there and eat and the parents tell us stories. 'Eat what I am telling you,' they said. 'Swallow all the information so you

Manuelita Lovato, artist,
Kewa Pueblo

can maintain it in your heart and you will always remember what you heard from us.' That's how we learned the stories of our history and our traditions."

Beauty abounds in Santo Domingo. But as with many Native communities, Santo Domingo Pueblo suffers from disproportionate rates of poverty and unemployment, chronic health conditions, and a lack of good-quality affordable housing. Unlike many Native communities, the Santo Domingo tribe has been living on this land for centuries, but the lack of housing has created overcrowding situations in which multiple generations often live in one home. Official counts vary, but 2017 US census data lists the reservation's population as 2,596,[2] while the state of New Mexico says more than 3,100 people live on the reservation,[3] and locals estimate that the true number may be as high as 5,000.

During his fellowship, Joseph helped design and develop Wa-Di, forty-one units of multifamily housing and a multiuse community center, in addition to working on a trading-post renovation and the development of a pedestrian corridor.

"Before I even got back on the plane after my interview, they called and said my life was going to change. Soon I was packing up my house in DC and driving through a snowstorm to Santa Fe."
—Joseph Kunkel

Designing culturally relevant homes for the Kewa people, who are deeply protective of their centuries-old culture, would take special care and consideration, since the community was justifiably leery of outsiders. But Joseph's background as a dual citizen of Native and nonnative communities gave him the credibility to act as a bridge between tribal residents and outside design teams as Wa-Di was being sketched. "I always looked at myself as an outsider," he says, "but I think because I was Native there were a lot of built-in similarities, like understanding the elder structure, deferring to your elders, and knowing your role. Being able to communicate between these two worlds" was crucial to a successful partnership.

So was candidly acknowledging missteps that had occurred in the past. "Historically, there were problems with trusting a tribal housing authority, because first of all there's simply not enough housing to go around," Joseph says. Some residents felt the whole system was rigged in some way. "'You don't provide housing to me,' or 'you're providing housing to your family first,' or 'you build crappy housing' were some of the prevailing narratives," he says. "So trying to address those issues and acknowledge those past faults in our community meetings was really important. Coming from a point of transparency and acknowledging that yes, we know there have been wrongs in the past, but we're here to move on from this point forward."

Tribal communities' distrust of outsiders' housing solutions is an extremely complex issue that goes back many decades. The Roosevelt-era Housing Act of 1937 enabled federally funded subsidies to be paid to local housing agencies, with the intention of providing "financial assistance . . . for the elimination of unsafe and unsanitary housing conditions, for the eradication of slums, [and] for the provision of decent, safe, and sanitary dwellings for families of low income."[4]

But as Joseph points out, "You can't really do that from DC. You can't develop housing that speaks to all of these [Native] communities across the country, because you're just going to place cookie-cutter homes all over. That's another kind of genocide in itself."

Wa-Di Housing Development, Santo Domingo, NM. Developer: Santo Domingo Housing Authority; Architect: AOS Architects

Aliza and Cianna Coriz,
residents, Wa-Di Village

Thousands of these cookie-cutter homes were built throughout Indian country, many with little heed to culture, climate, or geography, resulting in cheap, barracks-style housing that many communities associated with poverty and crime. They were completely at odds with Pueblo architectural and cultural typologies, which were communal and clustered.

At Ohkay Owingeh, for example, HUD housing was built on 100-by-100-foot lots separated by chain-link fencing, and the lack of access to conventional mortgage financing—not available until 1996 through the HUD 184 program—meant that the only recourse for tribal members who didn't qualify for a mortgage or were on a long waiting list was to purchase a trailer home. These homes immediately depreciated in value and, combined with poor government planning and lack of access to capital, kept many American Indian families from accumulating and passing on wealth.

The Native American Housing Assistance and Self-Determination Act of 1996 (NAHASDA) was enacted to remove some of the barriers to affordable, high-quality housing on Native American land and to recognize the right of tribal self-governance—which includes, as Joseph puts it, "tribes' ability to self-determine their own housing."

NAHASDA replaced several housing-assistance programs with a single block grant program.[5] But how does a tribe that has been denied self-determination for a hundred or more years know how to develop housing?

"You have an influx of capacity dollars, but you don't necessarily know how to manage those dollars, or you don't know that you need architecture and planning," Joseph points out. "You have outside contractors taking advantage of you. You have no building codes to adhere to. You have all these issues that come with development and construction for which you're not prepared. [The result] is another ten years of poor housing that isn't project managed. I liken it to another formula for self-destruction."

Little wonder, then, that Native communities distrust outsiders. Tomasita (Toma) Duran, executive director of the Ohkay Owingeh Housing Authority, recalls her tribe's initial resistance to the Tsigo Bugeh village project that was underway when Jamie came on the scene in 2000. "This was our first attempt to [use funding] other than our housing block grant, which was only $500,000," Toma says. "And this was the first time the tribe ever utilized tax credit resources. The tribe was very uncomfortable with the idea of an investor involved and funding 99 percent of the project, for a fifteen-year period. It took Jamie and me about two years to get them to a comfortable state where they allowed us to apply for the funding and develop the project."

Another first was being heard by a designer. "People were shocked that we were going to listen to them and adjust the design according to their feedback," Toma says. "For example, in the original design we had apartments on top of apartments. And they said, 'No, we don't want that. We need to be touching the ground. We have to have our feet on the ground.' So [the architects, Van Amburgh + Parés] changed the whole thing. It was also really important to have bigger kitchens and bigger living rooms so we could accommodate for feast days. Adjusting the design as we were listening to them had never, ever been done before."

It was through this community-based, adaptable design process that Toma realized for the first time "what NAHASDA was truly doing," she says. "It was allowing the flexibility tribes needed to develop housing according to their needs, which had never been done before."

More than a decade later at Santo Domingo, Joseph was facilitating a similar process at the Wa-Di Housing Development. Designed by AOS Architects, it includes forty-one units of multifamily housing and a 3,000-square-foot community center with a daycare, playground, basketball court, computer lab, and multipurpose space for community events.

At Wa-Di, "a lot of [the early work] was just talking through the design ideas and making sure the community was in charge of that process," he says, "and also conveying ideas so [community members] took them on themselves. All of that groundwork allowed us to talk about it as a *Santo Domingo* housing project, not just another cookie-cutter development."

A distinctly Santo Domingo housing development would reflect social cohesion and community. "Historically, Pueblo community development has been very concentrated," says Joseph. "Their social structure is very much like a city, where they're dependent upon one another, which I thought was very beautiful. I knew that if they were going to retain their culture, their community, and their social structures, their housing needed to reflect that."

With 75 percent of the community relying on the arts as their primary source of income, a top priority was studio space. And because many of the traditional processes for craft making, such as shell grinding, result in poor air quality, studios needed to be well ventilated and attached to, but separate from, the homes.

The original design was for twelve rental units, but when Greta Armijo, director of the Santo Domingo Housing Authority, came to New York for a Rose Fellow meeting and saw Via Verde, a beautiful, 225-unit, multifamily housing project that Jonathan Rose Companies developed, she worked with Joseph to change the design to forty-one units. The New Mexico Mortgage Finance Authority provided more than $9 million through Low-Income Housing Tax Credits and the Housing Trust Fund.

A mix of one-, two-, three-, and four-bedroom units, Wa-Di provides homes that are large enough for families, as well as one-bedroom units where young people can live independently while remaining rooted in the community. It is situated on more than 10 acres near the main village and the train station and historic trading post. All units are designed with passive solar orientation and built to Enterprise Green Communities Criteria. The development opened in 2017 and is fully occupied. "As soon as a unit was complete, people started moving in," Joseph says.

Among the residents are Cynthia Aguilar and Kewa jewelry maker John Lovato. Cynthia says her new home next to the community center and playground is "nice and roomy," with "lots of room compared to before," which comes in especially handy on Feast Day—and certainly helps with overcrowding on the reservation.

Manuelita, who is in her seventies, says that everyone her age "really, really understands" the extent of the overcrowding. "Sometimes it's two to three generations that live in one household," she says. Wa-Di provides "just enough room for people to be able to have privacy, but it's still a communal area," Cynthia says. "Most of the people that reside [here] participate or help in some way—all the energy is in the center."

NMRX

John Lovato, resident, Wa-Di Housing Development

John Lovato was born and raised on Santo Domingo. Starting at age five, he began learning jewelry making from his father, grandfather, and paternal uncles. After being laid off from a factory job in 2014, he "jumped into jewelry making" and now crafts turquoise jewelry full-time. John lived in the main village his entire life, but with no dedicated workspace of his own, he was forced to run extension cords from the house to an outside space next to a storage shed. At Wa-Di he has his own studio and enough room for his girlfriend and two children. In 2018, Wa-Di earned a Distinguished Architects Citation from the American Institute of Architects in New Mexico.

In addition to Wa-Di, Joseph took on two other major projects during his fellowship: Santo Domingo Heritage Arts Trail and the renovation of the community's historic trading post. In Santo Domingo fashion, they are all interconnected. "We knew housing alone wasn't going to solve the issues we saw in the community," Joseph says. With these three projects, however, "we had all the components from a planning standpoint that could stitch together and make up community."

The Santo Domingo Heritage Arts Trail was a response to the need for safe, attractive pedestrian access between the historic village and a nearby rail station running between Santa Fe and Albuquerque. The railway "connects the community to Santa Fe and Albuquerque and gives [residents] access to education, jobs, and food," Joseph says. "And, hopefully, brings people to the community" to patronize local businesses.

Joseph collaborated with residents, including Kewa artists, the Santo Domingo Tribal Housing Authority, SNCC, the landscape and urban design firm OLIN Studio, renowned artists Mary Miss and George Peck, and AOS Architects to design the 1.5-mile trail. Through an NEA Our Town grant, a Cultural District Plan was developed with community input—perhaps most notably, during the 2013 Santo Domingo Heritage Walk. During the event, more than a hundred community members, tribal leaders, and designers walked the trail and assessed the needs of the community, exchanging ideas relevant to the landscape and the culture and tribal history, and forging a collaborative vision for the community's future.

The new path, which connects the station with a new tribal artists' market and the Wa-Di housing development, honors Santo Domingo culture by featuring local artists' work. With the support of an ArtPlace grant, Mary Miss and George Peck served as artistic advisers and spent a year collaborating with local artists—among them Helen Bird, Connie Coriz, Manuelita Lovato, Thomas Tenorio, and master potter Robert Tenorio—who were hired to create sculptures that tell the tribe's story. Thomas played a key role in organizing local artists for the project. As an artist, Thomas has been able to give conservative Santo Domingo traditions a more modern spin, Joseph says.

Such a collaboration couldn't have happened without Joseph and Thomas bridging the divide between outsiders Mary and George and the Kewa artists, who are very protective of their traditions. Cynthia Aguilar kept a close eye on the proceedings to protect the tribe's privacy and sacred spaces. "It's very hard for any outsider to come in and make an impact," says George. "Yes, you are welcome on feast days, but to have any longer engagement is nearly impossible—every circumstance is difficult."

At first, Mary adds, "we weren't supposed to take pictures, draw anything, or ask questions." Slowly, over repeated visits, they were able to gain the trust of tribal members, and the most important cultural connector turned out to be the art itself. "George had done beautiful small-scale watercolors, and he shared those," Mary says. "This was something they could relate to."

George concurs. "At the beginning they were very suspicious, but over time, and after coming back again and relating 'artists to artists,' there was this incredible chemistry." The result was the production of six models that capture the vision of the tribal artists—and by extension, the entire community. "We were just there to guide them from an individual piece to doing something on a larger scale," says George. "We had a genuine desire to do something with them and learn from them. We learned a whole other world, and now Santo Domingo is very much in our hearts."

Manuelita Lovato's *Turquoise Lady* sculpture was based on a story her grandfather and father told her. "The Turquoise Lady came from the east with a basket full of turquoise," she says. "She walked down in front of the Santo Domingo Trading Post carrying that to the village, and she spilled the turquoise in the plaza. She told our people, 'These are your special gems that you will be working with. Produce them however you want. So that way you will always be enriched with things that will be coming to your reservation.' She's the one who brought the turquoise to us, so we respect her very highly and always talk about her."

Robert Tenorio treated an existing water tower as an iconic marker where the trail crosses the road; on the opposite side of the road, he and Connie Coriz designed a sitting area where Robert's paintings tell stories relating to the plants and animals in the region. In the center, Connie's artwork integrates contemporary Kewa design. Thomas Tenorio created an entry piece at the trailhead, 1.5 miles away from the village center, on the basis of Kewa shell design. Thomas Tenorio and Helen Bird designed a large Kewa pot that could be seen from the passing trains. The Heritage Trail is still in progress but close to completion, with sculptures and artwork remaining.

The Santo Domingo Trading Post is another success story. Built in 1922, it closed in the 1990s and was nearly lost to fire in 2001. The tribal planning department had raised the first $1.5 million before Joseph arrived and helped raise the final $1 million in renovation funds.

Its beneficiaries are local artists such as Rey Rosetta Pacheco and Farrell Pacheco, who make and sell traditional arts to support their family. Rey, a jewelry and clothing designer, and her husband, Farrell, who recently won Best in Class for jewelry at the prestigious Santa Fe Indian Market, moved back to Santo Domingo from Albuquerque after their children were born. "We wanted them to grow up here," says Rey. The family has a home and studio in the main village of Santo Domingo, and their self-sufficiency as working artists depends on customers having easy access to the pueblo.

The trading post is a work in progress. "As a tribal member I would like to see the trading post reopen soon," Cynthia Aguilar says. "I very much love this building. Everything about us is in the trading post. To me it's a living being, and I talk to it. It's part of how people made a living. When they grew crops or corn or grain, they'd bring it to the trading post and get their canned goods there, or whatever they needed. It sustained them." Cynthia hopes to write a children's book about it that will include

long the future Heritage Arts Trail

Farrell Pacheco, jeweler, Kewa Pueblo

Kewa history. "I'm thinking about the grandchildren," she says. "I want them to learn who they are. And I want us to have them see themselves on the shelf."

One reason for the delay is that the community hasn't yet agreed on how it will be run. The Santo Domingo practice of appointing a new tribal governor every year can slow progress, since leadership changes quickly and acting governors have relatively little time to bring initiatives to completion.

Throughout his time at Santo Domingo, Joseph continued to work with Jamie and Nathaniel at SNCC. "SNCC was always there," he says, "and I think the role they played during the fellowship was in taking what's going on in Indian country back to the nation, and vice versa. This is generational work, work that will take lifetimes. So how do we do that work justice, and how do we create precedents and share them with others who want to continue the work?"

One way is to practice the deep listening and empathy that occurs in every successful Rose Fellow partnership. Recently, I asked Jamie how she was able to enter Ohkay Owingeh as an outsider, and her answer was immediate: "With humility."

Joseph, Jamie, and Nathaniel approached their host communities with deep respect. They created SNCC only *after* being embedded with their respective host communities, listening to them, and witnessing the needs firsthand. All three former Rose Fellows remain involved in the recently formed Sustainable Native Communities Design Lab at MASS Design Group, a nonprofit architecture firm whose mission is to research, build, and advocate for architecture that promotes justice and human dignity.

Joseph, who was awarded a 2019 Obama Fellowship, is SNC Lab's director. Nathaniel Corum serves as its design director, and Jamie, who is now the executive director of the Santa Fe Art Institute, remains a MASS SNC Lab adviser and board member. Jamie also continues to serve the Ohkay Owingeh community as an Ohkay Owingeh Housing Authority board member, the only nonnative board member to date.

Joseph, Nathaniel, and Jamie have exhibited an uncommon ability to bridge boundaries—between traditional culture and modern design, between honoring Native communities' self-determination and the need for outside resources, and between knowing when to take a proactive role and when to empower community members to lead. They are committed to long-term collaborative work in Indian country and, whether they know it or not, are already inspiring the next generation.

Manuelita proudly reports that two of her former students are going to the University of New Mexico to study architecture. "I told them Joseph would be a good person to talk to, because he is a very good architect and a very good and knowledgeable person who has helped our people—a role model for our young people to look up to," she says. "I told them, 'Be sure and do that, because we don't have any architects from Santo Domingo! We need people like you to really get into it, so you can help our people—because our people need housing.'"

Only time will tell, but in just a few years Santo Domingo could produce its very first architects. And whether they choose to live on the reservation or live elsewhere and travel back and forth between two places, they will join a legacy of people working together to create the change they want to see in the place they call home.

Baltimore, Maryland

"It's a lot of good things that's going on in Baltimore City," says Donald Quarles, who has lived here for fifty years. "The news reporters are very keen on covering what's bad in Baltimore, but there is good. The good outweigh the bad, and we just have to share what's going on here."

In the summer of 2019, I traveled several times to West Baltimore's Franklin Square neighborhood to visit Rose Fellow Daniel Greenspan. Admittedly, my notions of Baltimore have been influenced by the dominant media narrative: an open-air drug market, one of the country's highest rates of death by gun violence,[1] abandoned lots, and failing public schools. And indeed, the challenges Baltimoreans face are real and urgent—the average life expectancy of residents in the neighborhood where Donald lives and Daniel works is just 68.3 years, and 38.5 percent live in poverty. But what's going on in Franklin Square is a shining example of what can happen when a handful of dedicated residents come together to save their neighborhood.

Something powerful is happening in West Baltimore, and if that story isn't yet making national headlines, it's because local activists—an intergenerational contingent cleaning up abandoned lots and fighting for better schools, safer streets, affordable housing, and economic opportunity—are just getting started.

Daniel, a native Floridian whose longtime aim has been to "speak social justice through the language of architecture," was hosted by the Bon Secours Health System in West Baltimore. The Sisters of Bon Secours (French for "good help") came to America from Paris in the late nineteenth century and established their first hospital in Baltimore in 1919. Their mission is to bring "healing, compassion, and liberation" to anyone in need.

"The sisters who founded Bon Secours would look at the work Daniel's engaged in, and they would say it's liberation, because it's liberating the potential of people," says George Kleb, Bon Secours executive director of housing and community development. "And the way to get to that liberation is through cocreating healthy communities."

Cocreation means listening to community members and working right alongside them to meet the needs they identify for their own neighborhood. If there is any distinguishing characteristic of what could be called "the Rose Fellow way," perhaps this is it. Daniel began his work in West Baltimore the way so many Rose Fellows do: by setting up community meetings and listening to residents' concerns and goals.

It was at a community charrette at Celebration Church on Monroe Street that Pastor Bob Washington introduced Daniel to Donald Quarles, a Franklin Square resident and

PEACE

Tavon Roundtree, West
Saratoga Street

NO PARKING
TUESDAY
TOW AWAY ZONE

Future site of the Kirby Lane Park

community activist. The two hit it off right away, finding common ground in their desire to take back the public space in West Baltimore. Donald, who moved with his family from Alabama to Baltimore in 1969 when he was nine years old, is motivated in part by memories of how Baltimore once was. He remembers a time when the neighborhood was primarily occupied by homeowners. The schools were good, the neighborhoods were clean, and the city offered summer camps and youth programs for kids.

"People cared about their homes; people cared about the property around them," he says. "People cared about trash being thrown out; people cared about everything. When I first came here Baltimore was beautiful, and that's why I want to see it progress, because I know what it can be."

Donald's neighbor, Franklin Square Neighborhood Association member Thelma Stokes, echoes those sentiments. "As a homeowner, you are proud of what belongs to you, and therefore you take care of it," she says. Thelma, seventy-six, has lived in Baltimore her entire life and remembers when mature trees lined the streets and the neighborhood was "simply elegant." This was the era of "the white marble steps," she says, and it was the job of the neighborhood children to scrub those steps weekly. "That was your first thing every Saturday morning," she says. "You got up and you scrubbed those marble steps until they were clean. They were so beautiful."

As the years passed, Thelma witnessed "a vast change" in her neighborhood. Like so many other blighted communities, the deterioration was the result of attitudes and policies that have a lot to do with perceptions about people and their value.

Beginning in the 1930s, redlining determined where minority communities could live, and denied them access to capital and investment—making community abandonment a matter of public policy. Though redlining has since been abolished, its effects linger. In Baltimore, for instance, research has found that neighborhoods redlined in the 1930s have lower rates of homeownership and college attainment, higher rates of poverty and segregation, and worse health outcomes overall.[2]

In the 1970s, Baltimore's economy shifted from industrial manufacturing to the service industry, and as factory jobs dried up, people began moving away. Those who did stay weathered harsh realities: soaring inflation, shuttered businesses, cuts to welfare and social services across the board, a national spike in homelessness after the release of patients from mental health facilities, and the crack epidemic of the 1980s.

"That's when the neighborhood really changed over," Thelma says. "Slum landlords came in and bought up the [vacant] properties for practically nothing" and then failed to care for their properties and, by extension, their tenants.

By 2000, as older people passed away or moved to senior housing, homeownership continued to fall. In some cases, young adults could not afford to take over their parents' homes, perhaps due to bad credit or the cost of needed renovations. Or maybe they simply didn't want the houses, since neighborhoods had become increasingly unsafe and schools progressively poorer.

Whatever the mix of factors, since the 1950s and '60s, homeownership has dropped steadily in these left-behind neighborhoods. When I visited the 1800 block of West Saratoga Street, where Donald lives, out of forty-two homes—which includes the corner lots of the neighboring streets—there were only eight owner-occupied houses.

Daniel Greenspan, Rose Fellow, 2017–2019

ald Quarles, resident,
st Saratoga Street,
imore, Maryland and
ounder, Kirby Lane Park

Seven houses have been demolished because of blight, and twelve were in imminent danger of being torn down. It is fair to say that all of the homes, whether owned by their residents or landlords, need significant repairs. But since the average house is valued at about $33,000, it's hard to see how those investments will pay off.

So—who cares about the 1800 block of West Saratoga Street? The businesses that would have cared are gone. Many of the landlords don't care. The city government, which has failed to bring basic services such as trash removal, street cleaning and maintenance, tree planting, sidewalk repair, and safety measures to the neighborhood, doesn't appear to care.

The residents surely do care, but it's easy to see how resignation sets in, and how difficult it is as an individual to know how to make a meaningful change in a system that disregards you. By any reasonable estimation, one could assume that the momentum of decline on 1800 West Saratoga Street was unstoppable. And yet, residents have taken matters into their own hands. They have grown tired of waiting for the city to act, tired of being told they must be patient. "We just don't have a lot of the basic infrastructure in terms of services that other places have," says George. "So the question is, How do you get the city to respond to issues that are important to people? Well, you create your own mechanisms."

What do people who care actually *do* when they're up against systemic forces of neglect? They start small—sometimes literally in their own backyards. At the community charrette where Donald and Daniel met, it emerged that the residents' primary concern was illegal dumping. The neighborhood had long been plagued by an accumulation of trash—from overflowing garbage bins that the city failed to empty as well as from outsiders using vacant lots as dumping grounds.

Daniel organized community meetings to get feedback from residents and strategize solutions. Together they came up with a plan "to do cleanups and stabilize the space," he says, "and prevent dumping with proactive measures such as fencing."

Ninety-five-year-old Mr. Willie was out every day, picking up trash. Donald emptied garbage bins, using his own trash bags. But two vacant homes in Franklin Square were scheduled for demolition, and neighbors knew what would happen next: the empty lots would become the sites of even more illegal dumping.

Donald and Daniel set about getting grant money to pay for fencing, and it quickly became apparent that they were a great team. "There's a chemistry there for sure," Daniel says. "There's a trust and a respect that makes it easy to work together."

Donald, true to form, is even more effusive: "Thank God for Daniel," he tells me. "Daniel's been an inspiration to this neighborhood. He really reached out and helps where he can help. Anything you ask him to do, he puts an effort in to try to do. We really appreciate what he's doing in the communities, not just the Franklin Square community, but any other community in the surrounding area. He's our hands-on."

By the summer of 2018, fences were installed around the vacant lots, which stopped the illegal dumping. This was a major neighborhood goal realized, but Donald and Daniel didn't want to just combat the negative—they wanted to build something positive for the community. "One of the things that's definitely going on here," Daniel says, "is we're carving out a territory that's for a different use. It takes a lot of energy,

Thelma Stokes with her grandchildren, Jason, Kimora , and Ty-Nia Terrell (left to right)

Lawrence La Prade, Officer,
Baltimore Police Department

Ronald Cobb, Kirby Lane Park

play
Franklin Square Community
play

planning, and consistency to keep those areas positive—because just as much energy and consistency is going in to keep them negative."

One of the first ideas for a positive gift to the community came from Donald, who wanted to revive a decades-old Franklin Square tradition of playing horseshoes. "Thirty years ago we started playing horseshoes on a vacant lot," he says. "Every weekend we'd be out there throwing horseshoes all day long, or sometimes after work until nightfall. We had a good time, a real good time. We started having tournaments, and everybody was out there playing, and laughing, and just enjoying each other."

"The community committed right away to the idea of putting in a horseshoe pit," Daniel recalls, "and then all sorts of other ideas started to develop too." Parents wanted a playground for their children. Thelma and other residents wanted more green areas—new trees and a place for seasonal and flower gardens. Neighbors wanted a barbecue pit, a place to share a meal, and a stage for musical performances.

Donald's vision built on those ideas. He had a deeper purpose in mind too: the new park would be a place of healing. "All of us have our hurts, habits, and hang-ups," he says, "and we all need healing." He wanted a serenity garden where people could come and meditate or just relax in a peaceful outdoor place and gain healing from a beautiful green environment, while children could play safely nearby.

"The serenity garden is 100 percent Donald, his vision and his spirit," Daniel says. "That's his heart and that's his heart connected to every single person. It's his way of offering a helpful way to get people from where he used to be to where he is."

"A lot of my work is simply about helping people have a voice and power in a city that isn't well situated to help them. It's building the capacity of community members to sit at a table when people are making decisions, and navigate it to what they want."
—Daniel Greenspan

Where he used to be is the same place so many others in West Baltimore found themselves: watching the decline of his neighborhood, struggling to maintain his family's home and sense of security. But the resilience Donald has shown throughout all of these challenges has given him strength. Unlike many residents, after his mother died in 2000, Donald and his wife chose to stay in the neighborhood. He credits his deep faith as his saving grace and guiding principle.

His sense of obligation to his community inspired him to take on a leadership role that he never anticipated. Through his church, Donald attended neighborhood meetings and got to know local activists and community development organizations and eventually became a block captain.

Franklin Square Neighborhood Association president Edith Gilliard says Donald has a knack for recruiting others to participate in his vision. "Taking on the responsibility as a leader, there are certain things you do," she says, "and one is getting others involved. Donald is good at that."

Meanwhile, Thelma laughs with evident pride when asked about Donald's evolving role in the community. "Oh, I've known him before he knew himself!" she says. "I've watched him grow up through the years, and I noticed how he began to take an interest. He's changed tremendously."

Work on the park Donald envisioned and Daniel helped design—called Kirby Lane Park after an adjacent alley—started with the installation of the horseshoe pit. People came out to play, and as word spread, more and more residents visited—to play horseshoes, to spend time with their neighbors, to see what was going on in this formerly neglected space.

Donald's infectious energy and charisma got other residents involved. Some cleared trash; others cleared weeds. Some brought tools and construction expertise. Some brought shrubs and perennials and helped plant them. Some brought food to neighborhood barbecues and working parties. Others brought ideas or encouragement or volunteer labor, pitching in wherever help was needed. Momentum built, and the work started to manifest itself in visible progress. The progress attracted the attention of more and more people, and then they got involved. All of this was fueled by the vision of a man who cared deeply.

Says Thelma, "Donald has my utmost respect, because [when he] realized the neighborhood was becoming an environment you really didn't want your children to live in, he didn't just talk about it; he took the initiative to get up and do something about it. If we had more like him, our inner city would be a lot better off—people who care."

Meanwhile, Daniel worked not only to plan and build the park, but to secure funding, meet city requirements, network with community organizations, and design a space that worked for this community. He helped plot the actions necessary to realize this shared vision. Through all the inevitable setbacks and delays, Daniel understood that while many discrete steps must happen to get from here to there, the spirit and motivations driving them are the magic that differentiates this project from so many others.

Kirby Lane Park opened to much fanfare in August 2019, the result of the work of multiple community groups, including Bon Secours, Celebration Church, Cunningham Recreation, Keep Baltimore Beautiful, the Parks & People Foundation, and Play for All, which donated playground equipment. Many dedicated volunteers showed up with a goal of finishing the playground construction within eight hours, and they did. The park has a slide and climbing equipment, a horseshoe pit, raised garden beds, and beautiful perennials, shrubs, and trees.

Kirby Lane Park is now used daily by adults and children and has become a living symbol of the revitalization people want for West Baltimore. Residents from other neighborhoods come to learn how the Franklin Square residents made this happen, and how they can build something similar in their own communities.

"People are amazed," Thelma says. "Some of the younger generation have never experienced a park like this; some of them have never been out of the inner city. The children I see going through here, they're astonished." So are the adults. "After they come down here and see this, they're like, 'Wow, we can do that?' Yes, it can be done! It just takes somebody to initiate, and I can't stop thanking Mr. Quarles enough for his initiative. That's what it takes—leadership. And now, just look how many people have become involved. We're revitalizing the neighborhood. This place brings back hope."

Kirby Lane Park is an ongoing labor of love. The crowning addition for Kirby Lane Park is a "serenity mural" depicting the Serenity Prayer and birds in flight, painted onto a gray wall that was left after the demolition. Donald's vision, as communicated

Rosa Wilkins, Celebration Church's Sunday service, Kirby Lane Park

GameTime
SOUTHWEST PARTNERSHIP
Franklin Square Community
Compass
CELEBRATION CHURCH

to artist Bridget Cimino, "will show how free the birds are and how they're able to be serene in different types of environments and different types of weather and accept the things they can't change, but have the courage to change the things they can," he says. "They always find a way to feed their babies; they always find a way to build a nest for their babies to live in."

Donald is moved by the birds because "they're small and have a lot to deal with, but they're so strong, and they're always thinking of what they can do next to survive in the elements."

Where others see a lack of hope, they see opportunity. "Baltimore is a city that's in crisis," says Donald, "but a city in crisis is a city that can see change. A city in crisis can be rebuilt in healthier ways. It doesn't have to be reduced to a couple of prevailing issues, such as drugs or crime. A city in crisis is a place where people can learn to love, rather than kill and destroy what's not theirs. A city in crisis is where a kid can learn there are better ways in life."

For Donald, Kirby Lane Park is just the beginning. He wants to save the houses that are at risk of being torn down so there won't be more empty lots in Franklin Square. He wants to take down the already-condemned houses and construct high-quality homes, with a daycare next door. He wants to plant street trees and beautify the block. And that's just on West Saratoga Street.

Donald's sentiments reflect an extraordinary attitude that I saw repeatedly in Baltimore—one of community pride, tenacity, and love. This attitude is growing, shepherded by ordinary neighbors motivated to provide time and labor and resources to restore their notion of the Beloved Community on their own blocks. And it's guided by dedicated partners such as Daniel, who contributed his skills not just to design and community development but to empowering the residents themselves.

"A lot of my work is simply about helping people have a voice and power in the design and development process which doesn't always prioritize either daily needs or passions, let alone demystify how things get done," Daniel says. "It's building the capacity of community members to have the ability to sit at a table when people are making decisions, and navigate it to what they want."

The lesson of West Baltimore is so clear. At the core of it is caring. All the mechanisms of community development—the grant programs, the funding streams, the services—can be deployed, but they are deployed only when enough people care enough to make that happen.

We need a revolution in caring, and what's going on at West Saratoga Street illustrates that caring deeply calls for a love that radiates past yourself and your family, and out into your community and into the larger world. It's the kind of care—of love—that can provide the motivation and means to get a small city park built—or, practiced at scale, that can change policy, financial structures, and the tools of design and development in order to revolutionize what it means to be at home in America.

"I want to live in Baltimore, and I want to get it back on the map," Donald says. "Baltimore is going to be a prime example of what can be if people just come together and work together. Baltimore can do it."

I believe him.

Mural: *Birds, Outdoor Adventures and Serenity*. Artist: Bridget Cimino, Kirby Lane Park

Serenit
Courag
Wisdom

Last Stop (for Now)

Over its twenty-year history, the Rose Fellowship has been a force of inspiration in the emergent field of public-interest design. Together, the fellows have changed how architecture and design are practiced. They recognize that any act of design is nested within a set of larger issues, and that one must know one's history and understand the larger systemic forces behind the issues to either reinforce or dismantle those systems.

They have demonstrated that "good design" is not in conflict with "social design," and indeed that design cannot be good if it is not legitimately improving some aspect of society. Architecture is not just a building or a design on a page. Architecture is a thing that makes you feel differently about your place in the world.

The last stop on this journey was Green River, Utah, population 952, as part of the fellows' retreat, which has become an annual tradition. Our host was Lindsey Briceno (2019–2020) and her organization Epicenter, a ten-year-old design center that helped create and implement Green River's housing plan in 2012.

In 2019, this retreat was both the same and different from what I experienced as a Rose Fellow in 2001. From a personal point of view, my toddler daughters had become young women, ages twenty-two, nineteen, and sixteen, pursuing their own missions, a testament not only to the passage of time, but a tangible reminder of how much we can learn and grow. In 2019, the twenty-one fellows in Green River were the largest cohort to date, reflecting the success of the program as it entered its twentieth year. They were there with partners from their host communities and supported by Enterprise Design Initiatives staff.

Still, some things remained the same. Our 2001 group learned from Tsigo Bugeh the importance of self-determination and how building a community engagement process built around storytelling can elevate shared values. This 2019 cohort was workshopping a prototype for a new Habitat for Humanity House to meet climate resilience challenges. And just as our 2001 group planned a weekend together in Chaco Canyon after the work week was done, this group organized a camping trip in Arches National Park after their retreat, carving out the personal time to build relationships.

Seven fellows, including Daniel Greenspan, were preparing to graduate and make their culminating presentations. I was spellbound as they spoke—by the amount of work accomplished, but also by the depth of relationships formed, the maturity

and confidence acquired, the humility of having learned so much more from their community than they felt they could possibly offer in return.

As I listened to this cohort of fellows and reflected on the stories told in this book, I thought about what we learn and how we learn. We learn from each other through stories, and I am so grateful to those who so kindly shared their journeys and lent their voices. They need to be heard.

And there are so many beautiful, unforgettable moments in each of the communities. Harry and I had been to San Ysidro many times, but it was thrilling for him to be photographing the opening of Living Rooms, a project that we anticipated for fifteen years. Atlanta helped us give a name—the Beloved Community—to our aspiration for this book project. In Thunder Valley, we watched the clouds roll in as Harry tried to capture the flash of a lightning bolt over the new houses. When I suffered a devastating personal loss, the staff of Thunder Valley sent me a beautiful handcrafted star quilt. Harry made a special trip back to Skid Row for the annual parade. We were in Yakima for apple-picking season and then back again when the apple blossoms were blooming. Seattle with Joann Ware was a culinary delight; we got to sample all of her favorite pastry shops and restaurants. Greenwood, Mississippi, feels like a home away from home with three Rose Fellows in residence. In Santo Domingo, Cynthia Aguilar taught us how to make tortillas—we ate them hot off the cast-iron skillet slathered with butter. And, of course, Baltimore. Harry, a native of the city, has made more than fifty trips to Kirby Lane Park, often with his camera, but sometimes just to plant bulbs. He sends me a text with the day's progress.

I am grateful for these moments. The challenges facing communities in America are overwhelming and unjust. The systems that maintain the status quo—that allow for racism, poverty, and homelessness to exist—are complicated and entrenched. But the beauty, power, and resourcefulness of the people who every day are striving to create their version of the Beloved Community are awe-inspiring. Let us be a part of that creative dedicated minority who will not rest until we make the world better.

Communities fare best when developers and designers work together, learning from each other. We need designers who can listen patiently, earning the trust of the people they serve. We need designers with fresh ideas and perspectives who can give vision and voice to a community's collective aspirations and needs.

We need those who can bring a high degree of respect and a willingness to learn the unique historical, political, economic, cultural, and social conditions of a place, especially if it is not their own. In turn, community groups can welcome designers and leverage their skills, sharing their values and methodology openly.

It is time for a new era for architecture, and I believe it is already at hand. One in which we will no longer question whether architecture can, or should, strive to achieve justice and excellence. One in which architects will no longer need to decide between doing well and doing good, since justice, dignity, and resilience will be built-in, nonnegotiable outcomes of design excellence. And one in which the entire design and development community will be organized around these collaborative principles and methods that rely on mutual listening, respect, and problem-solving. A community of practitioners that create design with a positive social impact.

Rose Fellows design by caring about what that experience is, not just for themselves and their families, or for their clients, but for every member of their communities, especially the most vulnerable. Rose Fellows are architects who design with love.

The time has come for us to actively resist designing new structures that rest on top of structural inequality. Instead, we must bring our whole selves to the effort of undesigning those very inequities.

This is what love looks like in design and community development. This is what it means to be a community architect. This is what the Rose Fellows are striving to do.

Endnotes

Introductory Quote

1. https://onbeing.org. Accessed December 2, 2019.

Introduction

1. https://www.c-ville.com.
2. https://dsl.richmond.edu.
3. https://www.povertyusa.org.
4. https://thekingcenter.org. Accessed September 2, 2019.
5. https://www.facebook.com/HarvardEducation. Accessed January 8, 2020.

San Ysidro, California

1. Area Median Income (AMI) is a series of income-level limits that households cannot exceed in order to be eligible for HUD-assisted housing. The lower the AMI percentage, the lower the household income, as measured against the midpoint income level of a defined geography. Households AMI levels are set annually by the US Department of Housing and Urban Development (HUD).

Atlanta, Georgia

1. https://www.nbcnews.com.
2. http://staging.aecf.org. Accessed November 18, 2019.
3. https://www.huffpost.com. Accessed November 18, 2019.
4. https://www.npr.org. Accessed November 18, 2019.
5. https://dsl.richmond.edu. Accessed November 24, 2019.
6. "Race and Economic Opportunity in the United States: An Intergenerational Perspective," by Raj Chetty, Nathaniel Hendren, Maggie R. Jones, and Sonya R. Porter. http://www.equality-of-opportunity.org.
7. EarthCraft is a green building program developed and administered by Southface. Its primary area of adoption is in the southeastern US. More information can be found at https://earthcraft.org.

Thunder Valley, South Dakota

1. https://www.census.gov. Accessed September 26, 2019.
2. https://www.re-member.org. Accessed September 26, 2019.
3. Ibid.
4. A grant-making program begun in 2016 by Enterprise Community Partners, Collaborative Action Grants of $5,000 are given to organizations to deepen community engagement and community placemaking/placekeeping through techniques that are participatory and culturally relevant.

Los Angeles, California

1. http://deptofplaces.org. Accessed December 24, 2019.
2. https://www.kcet.org. Accessed August 21, 2019.
3. Ibid.
4. Ibid.
5. https://99percentinvisible.org. Accessed August 21, 2019.
6. Ibid.
7. Ibid.
8. https://www.enterprisecommunity.org. Accessed December 16, 2019.
9. Supportive housing denotes affordable housing (typically serving persons who were recently experiencing homelessness) that is enriched with social services in the same building as their residence.

Yakima, Washington

1. https://factfinder.census.gov. Accessed September 11, 2019.
2. http://www.ncfh.org. Accessed September 10, 2019.
3. https://mhpsalud.org. Accessed September 11, 2019.

Seattle, Washington

1. https://www.historylink.org. Accessed December 3, 2019.
2. http://interimicda.org. Accessed September 17, 2019.
3. http://interimicda.org. Accessed December 27, 2019.

4. Evergreen Sustainable Development Standards (ESDS) is an affordable-housing green-building performance standard maintained by the Washington State Department of Commerce. More information can be found at https://www.commerce.wa.gov.
5. The LIHTC program is quite complex, and a full description lies well beyond the purview of this discussion. For those who wish to know more about its history as well as the current parameters of the program, please see the sources cited below, or refer to Alexander von Hoffman's excellent article, which can be found at www.jchs.harvard.edu. In this case, Enterprise was able to provide $11 million in LIHTC equity through investor Morgan Stanley.
6. http://sites.tufts.edu. Accessed September 17, 2019.
7. https://www.huduser.gov. Accessed September 17, 2019.
8. The Enterprise Green Communities Criteria ("the Criteria") was first developed in 2004 as the only green criteria specifically tailored to affordable-housing development. With input from users, the Criteria has been updated four times, with the latest edition released in 2020. The Criteria guides developers, designers, policymakers, and finance agencies on how to achieve their sustainability goals without significantly increasing the total development cost (TDC). The narrative in green building has long been that "affordable" and "sustainable" cannot coexist in the same housing product, but the Enterprise Green Communities Criteria challenges that notion by demonstrating that compliance with the Green Communities Criteria increases total development cost for new construction projects by as little as 2%, while increases to TDC for rehabilitation/renovation are under 1 percent.

   Enterprise took a strong position when it launched the Green Communities Criteria fifteen years ago. By developing a green-building standard with collaboration from the US Green Building Council, the National Resource Defense Council, and others, Enterprise put forth a bold vision that green, affordable housing was possible for all types of development, single family and multifamily, new construction and rehabilitation, in urban cities and rural communities alike. To date, the program has impacted more than 127,000 affordable homes nationwide; has leveraged more than $3.9 billion dollars in the development and preservation of green, affordable homes; and, at present counting, been included in twenty-seven states' funding requirements / incentive programs, making the Green Communities Criteria the most referenced sustainability program for affordable housing in the United States.

Mississippi Delta

1. https://www.locationshub.com. Accessed September 4, 2019.
2. https://www.fema.gov. Accessed September 9, 2019.
3. Gregory Flippins, personal interview, March 3, 2019. Delta Design Build Workshop conducted a roundtable conversation on housing issues in the Mississippi delta, inviting local experts such as Mr. Flippins to share their insights and experiences.
4. http://worldpopulationreview.com. Accessed September 5, 2019.
5. https://hopecu.org/manage/media/Eastmoor-One-pager.pdf. Accessed December 16, 2019.

Kewa Pueblo, New Mexico

1. https://www.arts.gov. Accessed October 9, 2019.
2. https://factfinder.census.gov. Accessed October 10, 2019.
3. https://www.newmexico.org. Accessed October 10, 2019.
4. https://babel.hathitrust.org. Accessed October 12, 2019.
5. https://www.hud.gov. Accessed December 16, 2019.

Baltimore, Maryland

1. https://www.washingtonpost.com. Accessed December 11, 2019.
2. https://www.twincities.com. Accessed October 23, 2019.

Acknowledgments

We are grateful to everyone in this book who welcomed us into their communities. Thank you for sharing your stories and allowing us to share ours.

For all the Rose Fellows, past, present, and future. I am as grateful for your passion, love, and humor as I am impressed by your talent, dedication, and hard work. Each of you has important stories to tell. For the fellows who are represented here, thank you for your vulnerability and courage.

Special thanks to all of the host organizations who have welcomed Rose Fellows and opened themselves to learning alongside them. We lost two heroes of community development recently, and honor the memory of Rick Goodemann (1953–2019), former executive director of Southwest Minnesota Housing Partnership, and Dean Matsubayashi (1969–2018), former executive director of Little Tokyo Service Center.

The Enterprise team—in the local offices and national headquarters—are among the most resourceful people I know. Special thanks to Melinda Pollack and Laurel Blatchford for their leadership and to the Boston-based design team Alma Balonen-Rosen, Kate Deans, Ray Demers, Jody Liu, Mark Matel, Carrie Niemy, Meghan Venable-Thomas, and Nella Young as well as Priscilla Almodovar, Susan Anderson, Jess Blanch, David Bowers, Russ Kaney, Judi Kende, Allison Knapp Womack, James Madden, Marion McFadden, Carmen Phelps, Meaghan Shannon-Vlkovic, and Michelle Whetten. Huge thanks to Enterprise alumni Dana Bourland, Amber Christofferson, Mary Hale, Matt Hoffman, Terri Ludwig, Taro Matsuno, Tom Osdoba, Mia Scharphie, Christopher Scott, Trinity Simons, Mayrah Udvardi, and Peter Werwath, all of whom have been instrumental to the success of the Rose Fellowship.

Jonathan Rose conceived of and launched this program in honor of his father, Frederick P. Rose, a gift that has reverberated through communities across America. Jonathan has been a personal mentor for me and, in his practice and writing, leads by example.

For the past twenty years, Enterprise's Rose Architectural Fellowship has been generously supported by a wide variety of local and national funders. These include (but aren't limited to) the Kendeda Fund, the Frederick P. & Sandra P. Rose Foundation, the Kresge Foundation, the Barr Foundation, the Surdna Foundation Inc., ArtPlace America, William Penn Foundation, Capital One, Evelyn & Walter Haas Jr. Fund, Freddie Mac Foundation, McKnight Foundation, the Richard H. Driehaus Foundation, Bullitt Foundation, Autodesk Foundation, Jonathan F. P. Rose, Knight Foundation, Fetzer Institute, Central Corridor Funders Collaborative / St. Paul Foundation, the Central Corridor Funders Collaborative / St. Paul Foundation, Fledgling Fund, the Cleveland Foundation, the Community Foundation for the National Capital Region, the George Gund Foundation, University of Minnesota Foundation Real Estate Advisors, America's FHL Banks, the Davis Family Foundation Inc., Bloomberg Philanthropies, California Community Foundation, Marshall L. and Perrine D. McCune Charitable Foundation, WinnCompanies, Saint Luke's Foundation, the Community Foundation of Western North Carolina, the Collins Foundation, and the George S. and Dolores Doré Eccles Foundation.

Diane Ives, from the Kendeda Fund, has been not only one of our most generous supporters, but also one of our most trusted advisers. When our first meeting in 2008 lasted over three hours, and Diane had learned each of the fellows' names and stories before the meeting, I knew she was an extraordinary funder—and person.

I am grateful for the opportunity to have been a part of the 2018–2019 cohort of Loeb Fellows at the Graduate School of Design at Harvard University. In my application, I asked the question "What will it take to make high-quality, affordable, beautiful housing a core human right?," and my exploration was around the concept that love and kindness could be critical tools of design. Thanks to the Loeb Fellowship Class of 2019 and faculty Alice Friedman, Christopher Herbert, David Luberoff, Jen Molinsky, Khalil Muhammad, John Peterson, Jim Stockard, Brandon Terry, Jonathan L. Walton, Terry Tempest Williams, and Sally Young for a heartfelt intellectual and academic investigation into love, home, citizenship, and equity.

Sincere thanks to Pete Schiffer and the team at Schiffer Publishing, especially Cheryl Weber, senior editor, whose commitment to high-quality affordable housing helped bring this book to fruition. Special thanks also to Catherine Knepper, who coached me through the writing of this book; Rebecca Bakken, who polished the manuscript; and book designers Amy Wilkins, Robin Brunelle, and Takaaki Matsumoto at Matsumoto Inc. for weaving together the narrative and photography.

And to my friends with whom the personal and the professional are one in the same—John Cary, April DeSimone, Martha McNamara, Kathryn Merlino, Michael Murphy, Walker Wells—thank you for helping me bring this book into the world. Kim Giangrasso, thanks for giving me shelter to write it!

And biggest love of all to my three daughters, Sophie, Olivia, and Bliss, who have grown up in the family of the Rose Fellowship. My work has also been our life, and they not only have tolerated my travel but also welcomed each class of new fellows into our home. I love you.

—Katie Swenson

As wonderful as it is to travel and take photographs across the USA, it's best to come home to my wife, Renee; my son, Wil and his Hayley; and Benny, who is always sad to see me go but so happy when I return. Dogs are like that.

Bob Tucker and Roger Lewin are valued sounding boards and better friends. And thanks and love to my sisters: Marion, Caroline, Anne, Eileen, and Rosemary—the Connolly Clan.

There is one more group to thank—the Rose Fellows. They have become family and, very often, friends to me. It's my great fortune to know them.

—Harry Connolly

Biographies

Katie Swenson is a nationally recognized design leader, researcher, writer, and educator. Katie is senior principal at MASS Design Group, a nonprofit design collective that designs, builds, and advocates for architecture that promotes human dignity. She was formerly vice president of eesign & sustainability at Enterprise Community Partners, a national nonprofit that has invested $43.6 billion in community development since 1982. The Enterprise Rose Fellowship has been showcased at the Museum of Modern Art, the Cooper-Hewitt National Design Museum, the New York Center for Architecture, and the National Building Museum, and recognized by the American Institute of Architects for its groundbreaking work. She is the coauthor of *Growing Urban Habitats: Seeking a New Housing Development Model* and the author of *In Bohemia: A Memoir of Love, Loss, and Kindness*.

Harry Connolly has been a photographer since age five. Documenting people's stories is a privilege he never takes lightly. He is the author of *Heading Home: Growing Up in Baseball* and *Fighting Chance: Journeys through Childhood Cancer*. Harry has been on the *Today Show*, *CBS Sunday Morning*, and NPR, and his photos have appeared in many magazines and been used by many clients. Home is Baltimore, but his work takes him across the US.

Rose Fellows

2000–2003
Dan Adams
Asian Neighborhood Design
San Francisco, CA

Peter Aeschbacher
Los Angeles Community Design Center
Los Angeles, CA

Jamie Blosser
Ohkay Owingeh Housing Authority
Ohkay Owingeh, NM

Steve Hoffman
Hale Empowerment & Revitalization Organization
Greensboro, AL

2001–2004
Colin Arnold
Community Housing Partners Corporation
Christiansburg, VA

David Flores
Casa Familiar
San Ysidro, CA

Parie Hines
Delridge Neighborhoods Development Association
Seattle, WA
Andy Schneggenburger
The Historic District Development Corporation
Atlanta, GA

Katie Swenson
Piedmont Housing Alliance
Charlottesville, VA

2003–2006
Victoria Ballard Bell
Design Corps
Raleigh, NC

Nathaniel Corum
Red Feather Development Group
Bozeman, MT

Michael Gatto
Foundation Communities
Austin, TX

Fernando Marti
Neighborhood Design, Mission Housing Development Co.
San Francisco, CA

Jess Zimbabwe
Urban Ecology
Oakland, CA

2005–2007
Andy Brookes
Harlem's Congregation for Community Improvement
New York, NY

Tara Siegel
Pratt Center for Community Development
New York, NY

Noel Toro
LINC Housing Corporation
Long Beach, CA

Steven Utz
Crawford County Coalition on Housing Needs, Inc.
Meadville, PA

2005–2008
Joshua Galloway
Better Housing Coalition
Richmond, VA

Ben Gates
Central City Concern
Portland, OR

Katherine Williams
Visitación Valley CDC & San Francisco Housing Dev. Corp.
San Francisco, CA

Spencer (Haynsworth) Woodcock
Santa Fe Community Housing Trust
Santa Fe, NM

2007–2010
Carey Clouse
Providence Community Housing
New Orleans, LA

Jessy Ledesma
Farmworker Housing Development Corporation
Portland, OR

Ophelia Wilkins
Regional Housing Alliance, Colorado Housing, Inc.
Pagosa Springs, CO

Esther Yang
Fordham Bedford Housing Corporation
Bronx, NY

2008–2011
Abbie Loosen
Project for Pride in Living (PPL)
Minneapolis, MN

Laura Shipman
Community Housing Partnership
San Francisco, CA

Seth Welty
Gulf Coast Community Design Studio
Biloxi, MS

2009–2012
Theresa Hwang
Skid Row Housing Trust
Los Angeles, CA

Daniel Splaingard
Bickerdike Redevelopment Corporation
Chicago, IL

2010–2013
Juan Calaf
ENLACE/PathStone
San Juan, PR

Wayne Mortensen
Neighborhood Progress, Inc.
Cleveland, OH

Joann Ware
InterIm CDA
Seattle, WA

Jason Wheeler
Color Country Community Housing, Enterprise Community Partners
Saint George, UT; New York, NY

2012–2014
Sam Beall
Cathedral Square Corporation
Burlington, VT

Sam Carlsen
Saint Paul Riverfront Corporation
Saint Paul, MN

Mark Matel
Nuestra Comunidad Development Corporation
Boston, MA

Ceara O'Leary
Detroit Collaborative Design Center
Detroit, MI

Nathan Poel
Office of Rural and Farmworker Housing
Yakima, WA

2013–2014
Cesia Lopez-Angel
Little Tokyo Service Center & Neighborhood-Based CDC Coalition
Los Angeles, CA

2013–2015
Geoffrey Barton
Mountain Housing Opportunities (MHO) & Asheville Design Center
Asheville, NC

Emily Roush-Elliott
Greenwood-Leflore Economic Development Corporation
Greenwood, MS

Joseph Kunkel
Santo Domingo Housing Authority and Sustainable Native Communities Collaborative (SNCC)
Santo Domingo, NM

2014–2015
Esteban Reichberg
CAMBA Housing Ventures
Brooklyn, NY

Shelly-Anne Tulia-Scott
Presbyterian Senior Living
Dillsburg, PA

2014–2016
Michael Chavez
Fairmount Indigo Line CDC Collaborative
Boston, MA

James Lewis
Heartland Alliance
Chicago, IL

Hilary Noll
First Community Housing
San Jose, CA

Erick Rodriguez
Burten Bell Carr Development, Inc. & Detroit Shoreway Community Development Organization
Cleveland, OH

2015–2017
James Arentson
Southwest Minnesota Housing Partnership
Slayton, MN

Joshua Budiongan
Jefferson East, Inc.
Detroit, MI

Brita Carlson
A Community of Friends (ACOF)
Los Angeles, CA

Stephen Klimek
The Cornerstone Group
Minneapolis, MN

Annie Ledbury
East Bay Asian Local Development Corporation (EBALDC)
Oakland, CA

Alexis Smith
Jewish Community Housing for the Elderly (JCHE)
Brighton, MA

2016–2017
Allan Co
Hudson River Housing
Poughkeepsie, NY

Jae Shin
New York City Housing Authority (NYCHA)
New York, NY

Ai-Lien Vuong
Denver Housing Authority
Denver, CO

2016–2018
Jess Blanch
Capitol Hill Housing
Seattle, WA

Kaziah Haviland
Thunder Valley CDC
Porcupine, SD

Irene Figueroa Ortiz
A Better City
Boston, MA

2017–2019
Kristen Chin
Urban Edge & Jamaica Plain Neighborhood Development Corporation (JPNDC)
Boston, MA

Daniel Greenspan
Community Works and Unity Properties at Bon Secours Hospital
Baltimore, MD

Kelsey Oesmann
Urban Housing Solutions
Nashville, TN

Lea Oxenhandler
People's Emergency Center (PEC) Community Development Corporation
Philadelphia, PA

Nicholas Satterfield
New Orleans Redevelopment Authority (NORA)
New Orleans, LA

Michelle Stadelman
Community and Shelter Assistance (CASA) of Oregon, Hope Enterprise Corporation & Delta Design-Build Workshop
Sherwood, OR; Greenwood, MS

2018
Jason Minter
[bc]WORKSHOP
Houston, TX

2018–2019
Delma Palma
New York City Housing Authority (NYCHA)
New York, NY

2018–2020
Nicholas Forest
Quest Community Development
Atlanta, GA

Dawn Hicks
Venice Community Housing
Los Angeles, CA

Seema Kairam
The Trust for Public Land
St. Paul, MN

2019
Emily Thompson
Burten, Bell, Carr Development, Inc.
Cleveland, OH

2019–2020
Lindsey Briceno
Epicenter
Green River, UT

Deborah Lin Pérez Centeno
Atlanta Habitat for Humanity
Atlanta, GA

Chau Pham
Ithaca Neighborhood Housing Services (INHS)
Ithaca, NY

2019–2021
Siboney Díaz-Sánchez
Opportunity Communities (OppCo)
Boston, MA

Alicia Ginsberg
Rosebud Economic Development Corportation (REDCO)
Mission, SD

Nick Guertin
Coalfield Development
Wayne, WV

Haley Hardwick-Witman
ONE Neighborhood Builders
Providence, RI

A.L. Hu
Ascendant Neighborhood Development (AND)
New York, NY

Yuko Okabe
North Shore CDC
Salem, MA

Olivia Jiménez
Foundation Communities
Austin, TX

Carol Zou
Little Tokyo Service Center
Los Angeles, CA

Other Schiffer Books by Katie Swenson:
In Bohemia: A Memoir of Love, Loss, & Kindness, 978-0-7643-5997-2

Other Schiffer Books on Related Subjects:
Housing and the City: Love versus Hope, Daniel Solomon, 978-0-7643-5643-8

Library of Congress Control Number: 2020930571

Creative direction by Takaaki Matsumoto, Matsumoto Incorporated, New York
Designed by Robin Brunelle, Matsumoto Incorporated, New York

Typeset in William and Interstate

ISBN: 978-0-7643-5993-4
Printed in China

Published by Schiffer Publishing, Ltd.
4880 Lower Valley Road
Atglen, PA 19310
Phone: (610) 593-1777; Fax: (610) 593-2002
E-mail: info@schifferbooks.com
Web: www.schifferbooks.com

Front endpaper: Mural: *Where the Southern Crosses the Yellow Dog*; Artists: Mayor George Holland and wife, Johnna Holland, Moorhead, MS
Opposite: Shuri of Wakanda and James Arther (pseudonyms), residents, Downtown View, Minneapolis, a project of Abbie Loosen, Rose Fellow 2008–2011. Developer: Project for Pride in Living (PPL) and Youthlink; Architect: UrbanWorks Architecture
Back endpaper: Thunder Valley, Pine Ridge Reservation, Porcupine, SD

ARE
HOME

Thatȟánka Iyotaka Ave